ELIZABETH BISHOP was born in Worcester, Massachusetts, in 1911 and graduated from Vassar College in 1934. She traveled widely as an adult, living in Paris, Mexico, New York, Florida, and, for more than a decade, Brazil, before returning to the United States. Her work was immensely prized for its distinctive clarity, precision, and depth, and she was awarded the Pulitzer Prize, the National Book Award, and the National Book Critics Circle Award, among others. Over time she has come to be acknowledged as one of America's essential poets. She died in Boston in 1979.

WILLIAM BENTON is the author of eight books of poetry and a novel, *Madly* (2005). He curated the first exhibition of Elizabeth Bishop's artwork at the East Martello Tower Museum in Key West in 1993. He lives in New York.

ALSO BY ELIZABETH BISHOP

North & South (1946)

A Cold Spring (1955)

The Diary of "Helena Morley" (translation) (1957)

Brazil (with the editors of *Life*) (prose) (1962)

Questions of Travel (1965)

The Ballad of the Burglar of Babylon (1968)

The Complete Poems (1969)

An Anthology of Twentieth-Century Brazilian Poetry (edited with Emanuel Brasil) (1972)

Geography III (1976)

The Complete Poems: 1927–1979 (1983)

The Collected Prose (1984)

One Art: Letters (1994)

Edgar Allan Poe & The Juke-Box: Uncollected Poems, Drafts, and Fragments (2006)

Elizabeth Bishop: Poems, Prose, and Letters (2008)

Words in Air: The Complete Correspondence Between Elizabeth Bishop and Robert Lowell (2008)

Prose (2011)

Poems (2011)

Elizabeth Bishop and The New Yorker (2011)

ELIZABETH BISHOP

EXCHANGING HATS

PAINTINGS

EDITED AND WITH AN INTRODUCTION AND AFTERWORD

BY WILLIAM BENTON

FARRAR, STRAUS AND GIROUX

NEW YORK

ACKNOWLEDGMENTS

The forty-two works by Elizabeth Bishop reproduced in this book are all that are currently known. In number they are equal to over a third the total number of poems that she released for publication.

An attempt at chronology has been made; however, so many pictures are undated that it is less a chronology than a division into—with a few exceptions—three basic periods: New York (1934–37), Key West (1938–48), and Brazil (1951–67).

I am extremely grateful to Alice Methfessel for wise advice and great generosity. I would also like to thank Angela Leap, Loren MacIver, Frani Blough Muser, Cynthia Krupat, Dorothee Bowie, Margaret Miller, Robert Giroux, and Nancy MacKecknie, Curator of Rare Books and Manuscripts, Vassar College Library. I would especially like to thank Alice Quinn for support and guidance, and Rust Hills for making this project possible in the first place.

ACKNOWLEDGMENTS TO THE SECOND EDITION

Thanks are due to Ron Patkus, Head of Special Collections, Vassar College, and to Dean Rodgers and Laura Finkel for their generous help in making the Vassar collection of Bishop's pictures available; to James Jaffe at James Jaffe Rare Books, Marie Evans at Alexandre Gallery, John Wronoski at Lame Duck Books, and Cynthia Krupat for providing digital images of a number of paintings; and to Natsuko Kinoshita for invaluable help.

Farrar, Straus and Giroux
18 West 18th Street, New York 10011

Distributed in Canada by D&M Publishers, Inc.
Printed in Great Britain
Originally published in 1996 by Farrar, Straus and Giroux
This revised paperback edition originally published in 2011 by Carcanet Press, Great Britain
First American paperback edition, 2011

The Library of Congress has cataloged the hardcover edition as follows:
Bishop, Elizabeth, 1911–1979
Exchanging hats : paintings / Elizabeth Bishop ; edited with an introduction by William Benton. — 1st ed.
p. cm.
1. Bishop, Elizabeth, 1911–1979—Catalogs. 2. Authors as artists—Catalogs. I. Benton, William. II. Title.

ND237.B5939A4 1996
759.13—dc20

96007963

Paperback ISBN: 978-0-374-53343-4

www.fsgbooks.com

1 3 5 7 9 10 8 6 4 2

CONTENTS

INTRODUCTION

One evening my friend Rust Hills told me about an Elizabeth Bishop seminar he was helping to organize. It was scheduled to take place in Key West, where Bishop had lived from 1938 to 1948. Her house on White Street was to be designated a national literary landmark; several poets and writers had been invited to participate in readings, lectures, and panel discussions – among them Richard Wilbur, Anthony Hecht, Mark Strand, James Merrill, Elizabeth Hardwick, and Nobel Prize laureate Octavio Paz. When I asked if Bishop's paintings would be on view, Rust said that he'd seen nothing in the seminar's program that made any reference to her paintings; in fact, he hadn't been aware that Elizabeth Bishop was a painter. I, too, was unfamiliar with Bishop as a painter, but I had seen on the dust jackets of recent books three reproductions of her watercolors. A certain level of accomplishment, as well as public dissemination, seemed obvious. And yet, if that was true, how could an occasion honoring Elizabeth Bishop fail to acknowledge what was apparently a significant aspect of her achievement? It was puzzling. At Rust's request, I agreed to look into the status of Bishop's art and, if possible, put together a show of her paintings for the Key West seminar.

As it turned out, the exhibition took place at the East Martello Tower Museum in Key West, from January 7 to February 7, 1993. It marked the first time that a collection of Bishop's work had been shown. The art world had never heard of her. I later discovered that two of her pictures had been hung in a show of paintings-by-writers at the Arts Club of Chicago in 1971; aside from that, she had never been affiliated with a gallery. To assemble a group of her paintings meant not just securing their loans but finding them first. There was also the question of whether there were enough pictures to make up a show.

The process of tracking the paintings down, and of eventually putting on the exhibition, led through a community of her friends. They were all a little like characters in the same novel – generous, helpful, at times vivid, and most of them now in their seventies and eighties. Once, inquiring about a picture, I was told it had been stolen following the death of the person who owned it. Mildly arcane clues were proffered as to who had taken it; when I guessed the name, a tittering admonishment was uttered: "You didn't hear it from *me!*" The seminar itself was marked by the florescence of a whole new generation of Bishop fans. John Malcolm Brennin, one of the gatekeepers of Bishop's reputation, wrinkled his brow and intoned, "Who are all these poor relations of Elizabeth's?"

Cynthia Krupat, a leading book designer at Farrar, Straus and Giroux, had designed Bishop's *Complete Poems: 1927–1979* and *Collected Prose*; each had a Bishop watercolor reproduced on the jacket. Another watercolor had been used for the jacket of a critical work about her poetry, published by Columbia University

Press, listing Vassar College Library as its source. No source was listed on the Farrar, Straus and Giroux books, but Cynthia explained that they, too, had been made from slides in the collection at Vassar. During our conversation, I mentioned that I hoped to acquire works from private collections as well, and would appreciate any leads she could give me. She couldn't think of anybody who owned one, but then she added – "except for my mother."

Cynthia Krupat's mother, Frani Blough Muser, was Elizabeth's oldest friend. They met at the Walnut Hill boarding school when Elizabeth was sixteen. Frani's portrait of Elizabeth at school has become a staple quotation in writing about Elizabeth Bishop: "She looked remarkable, with tightly curly hair that stood straight up, while the rest of us all had straight hair that hung down . . . We called her 'Bishop' . . . and we all knew with no doubt whatsoever that she was a genius." When I spoke with Frani (not Franny; it rhymes with "rainy"), she readily agreed to lend her painting. She wanted to know the opening date of the exhibition. As an approximate date, I offered the first of January. "New Year's Day?" she asked with an alert incredulity. I admitted that an exact date hadn't really been set, and then remarked that perhaps they didn't have New Year's in a place like Key West. "Only old years," she said.

Robert Giroux, Elizabeth's friend and publisher, provided the names of several people to contact, among them the painter Loren MacIver. At her studio on Perry Street, which Bishop often visited and where she sometimes stayed, Loren MacIver, in a quilted jacket with a wrist scarf tied to one sleeve, was still, in her eighties, a working artist. We sipped non-alcoholic champagne and she quoted passages from Joyce, while her assistant brought out recent canvases of Loren's. "This studio looks like the last act of *La Bohème,*" she proclaimed. There was a painting by E.E. Cummings on the wall, and a small Calder sculpture made out of the wire lace of a champagne cork. Finally she showed me her Bishops – two watercolors. (She later found two more paintings and two drawings, which she had forgotten she owned.)

At Vassar College Library, in their Special Collections, I found twelve paintings. They were loose in folders, unmatted, on fragile paper that in some cases was frayed and torn at the edges. They looked like pressed butterflies. Even if no other paintings were found, this would bring the total to fifteen and would be enough for a small show. Notably missing from the Vassar collection were the pictures which had been used for the three cover illustrations. They were, however, represented there in a group of slides (from which the covers had been reproduced) along with slides of another seventeen paintings which Vassar could not account for.

Alice Methfessel, Bishop's companion and the executor of her estate, was much younger than Elizabeth, tall in a photograph, and, by numerous accounts, formidable. Pronouncing her name made you lisp. She lived in San Francisco and owned several of Elizabeth's paintings. "The *best* ones," she said. We spoke by phone and she gave her provisional approval to the project and invited me to California to look at the pictures in her collection. Alice was gracious and accommodating, helping to photograph the paintings, providing details and footnotes to various aspects of Elizabeth's work and, with her friend Angela Leap, wining, dining, and touring me around the city in their convertible ("San Francisco is an aphrodisiac; New York is a vitamin").

Of the three jacket illustrations I had been looking for, two were among the eleven pictures beautifully framed and hung all in a row along one wall at Alice's house. The third – the *Tintin*-like interior of a ship's cabin with an open porthole view of the sky and blue sea – remains lost. Another painting – not represented in any of the slides or other references – turned up in Seattle. Other investigations led literally to dead ends – people whose pictures had vanished after they died and left no heirs.

By this point, a total of twenty-seven paintings and drawings had been enlisted for the Key West exhibition. That left ten others, whose whereabouts were unknown, identified by slides. Some of these were obviously in Brazil, where Bishop had lived for twenty years, and lay beyond the scope and resources of the project.

And then there was Margaret Miller's picture. Miller, a friend and Vassar classmate of Elizabeth's, was herself a painter. In 1937 she lost part of her right arm in a car wreck when she, Bishop, and Louise Crane were driving from Burgundy to Paris. She had at one time worked at the Museum of Modern Art. "Difficult" was a word – muted in a sigh – that kept turning up to describe her. I first telephoned her when I began the search for Elizabeth's paintings. She spoke in a frail voice, marked by long pauses as she lost and recovered her breath. But her response to the idea of a show of Elizabeth's work was positive; she had a painting; she would be happy to lend it to the exhibition. It was agreed that I would personally take care of crating and shipping the picture. I asked when it would be convenient for me to pick it up. There was a long pause. "You can't come here," she said firmly.

"How will I get the picture?"

"I don't know," she said.

As I was later to find out from friends of hers, she allowed no one to visit her apartment. We had several conversations over the next few months, always pleasant, each ending in more or less the same stalemate. She considered leaving the painting with Frani Muser, but then decided not to. At other times, when we spoke, the sheer logistics of the dilemma proved wearying and insurmountable; messenger services and all other suggestions were rejected. I decided against trying to borrow the painting for the show. It was, after all, only one painting and not worth creating unnecessary hardships for someone in Miller's circumstances. I once said to her I was willing to accommodate whatever exigencies were involved in facilitating the loan of the picture. Her response was, "All my exigencies are permanent."

In December, as the deadline for the show arrived, I called Miller once more. I now knew which picture was hers. The elliptical descriptions she had given of it matched one of the slides in the "whereabouts unknown" group. To confirm it, I'd sent her a little sketch of the picture. (She replied that I had "flubbed the turrets.") It was a particularly fine painting of the Key West Armory building, palms peeking out from behind it, an overcast sky reflected in windows bordered by blue shutters. (Curiously, in a town of enchanting "piano-box houses," as Wallace Stevens called the Key West architecture, Bishop painted primarily its large public buildings.) Miller, as usual, assented to the "idea" of lending her picture to the exhibition. The impasse of achieving this had become a recurring absurdity, but I again offered to do whatever I could to make it happen. Genuinely trying to find a solution, she proposed that we meet at Grand Central Station. I accepted; she then reconsidered, because the idea was "a little unsavory." I suggested that we meet somewhere in her neighborhood; she was too tired to think at the moment, she explained, and would have to hang up.

Around eleven o'clock that night, the doorman in my building notified me that a package had arrived. It was Margaret Miller's painting, unframed and meticulously wrapped. Freezing rain was blowing in the streets; she lived in lower Manhattan and my apartment was on the Upper West Side. The doorman described the woman who had delivered the package as tall, thin, elderly, and nice-looking. It was Margaret Miller.

In "Love Lies Sleeping," a poem written in her early twenties, Bishop sees a city from a window:

an immense city; carefully revealed,
made delicate by over-workmanship,
detail upon detail,
cornice upon facade,

reaching so languidly up into
a weak white sky, it seems to waver there.

Then she turns the real city into an imaginary city:

(Where it has slowly grown
in skies of water-glass

from fused beads of iron and copper crystals,
the little chemical "garden" in a jar
trembles and stands again . . .

And then she paints it:

pale blue, blue-green, and brick.)

The poem mimes the making of a watercolor. And in a life where travel (and fabulous cities) played such a significant role, watercolors – almost as portable as poems – seem appropriate.

Meyer Schapiro, the distinguished art critic, said, "She writes poems with a painter's eye." Bishop quotes this in a 1966 interview, and then continues, "I was very flattered . . . I'd love to be a painter." Painterliness itself, or what is so often seen to be painterly in writers – lyric detail anchored in observation, etc. – is, of course, a poetic given, a kind of *meubles.* (Jorge Luis Borges imagined an aesthetics in which it was tacitly understood that *every* poet was able to write the most beautiful line in the world.) In Bishop's poems, decorative surfaces exist here and there but – like the use of traditional genre and rhyme – remain formal decisions tied to specific contexts and not an overall literary intention. Her eye discriminates a hierarchy of values. Much of what is visual in her poetry happens at a structural level; it is part of the poem the way consciousness of sight is part of sight, and forms an integral ("a blue and brown river") that persists throughout her work.

In "The Map," the first poem in her first book, an actual map with its schemata of colors, "more delicate than the historians'," serves as a "map" for the composition of the poem she is writing. The two-dimensional object becomes a system of poetic notation, as the poet's voice carries us into the wit and complexity of a three-dimensional world:

The shadow of Newfoundland lies flat and still.
Labrador's yellow, where the moony Eskimo
has oiled it.

Her poem "Large Bad Picture" takes for its "map" an oil painting by her great-uncle. "From the Country to the City" uses topographical facts of a real landscape. Thirty years later, the epigraph of *Geography III,* itself a found object, diagrams the vectors of a compositional map, and "Poem," from that collection mediates between

art "copying from life" and life itself . . .

In "The Man-Moth," images are collaged onto the dark background of New York City:

Up the facades,
his shadow dragging like a photographer's cloth behind him . . .

In "Over 2,000 Illustrations and a Complete Concordance," the calm compass of the poem moves between pictures in a book and scenes of real life, until the end of the poem approaches a dimension beyond the inventories of the eye:

Open the heavy book. Why couldn't we have seen
this old Nativity while we were at it?
— the dark ajar, the rocks breaking with light,
an undisturbed, unbreathing flame,
colorless, sparkless, freely fed on straw,
and, lulled within, a family with pets,
— and looked and looked our infant sight away.

And in "The Moose," memory colors with the transparency of watercolor scenes from Nova Scotia as, in her mature voice, the natural order of words becomes the primary artifice by which things are made visible to our imagination:

. . . the fog
shifting, salty, thin,
comes closing in.

It's cold, round crystals
form and slide and settle
in the white hens' feathers,
in gray glazed cabbages,
on the cabbage roses . . .

If Elizabeth Bishop wrote like a painter, she painted like a writer. All her paintings are small, on sheets of paper the same size that one might write a poem on. The earliest-dated work is the 1937 portrait, *Sha-Sha.* Most of the pictures are undated. *Red Flowers on Black* (summer of '77 or '78) is probably the latest. Bishop died in 1979, at the age of sixty-eight.

In 1971 she said, "From time to time I paint a small gouache or watercolor and give them to friends . . . They are Not Art – NOT AT ALL." They are, though. They are just not to be confused with a process whose order and intensity penetrates the matrix of a life. Her paintings were done differently; her life entered them. They were the product and occupation of leisure, of fiddling around when more important work was out of the way or out of the question. She used poor materials, paper that traveled light and then disintegrated. Her method for the most part consisted of making a simple drawing and, unceremoniously, coloring it in. And yet if she was, as she called herself, a "genuine primitive," she also understood from the beginning that intrinsic value inheres in the grace of enactment and not in the obligation to closely approximate. She was, as David Kalstone said, "aware of the smallness and dignity of human observation."

At her best, limitations of technique are brightly revised into elegant solutions. The amateur makes marks that deliver an unplanned freshness to the composition – single strokes of palm leaves or the red patterns sketched on a tablecloth at an angle to the picture plane. The paintings can never be more than a partial account of their virtue. She was enough of a New Englander to interpret this as an advantage. The horizontal pencil lines on the façade of *The Armory, Key West* are as self-aware in their way as an Agnes Martin. A monumental symmetry invests *Harris School,* softened by playful kites and a bicycle lying on its side, which half-rhymes with the two rock-encircled trees. *Sleeping Figure,* with its headboard of inverted commas, is wonderfully organized around a series of rectangles. Beneath the kimono-clad figure, a blanket covers the bed, exact and tactile in its accuracy, the delicately mixed brown and neutral tones set off by the pun of a red book, which recalls the soft left-on reading light. She liked Klee, Vuillard, bought a Schwitters, and glanced at – one would bet – Hergé. But she is her own best influence; her paintings are like her poems, and made with the same, if lesser, powers. In *E. Bishop's Patented Slot-Machine,* a rainbow arc with the legend "The 'Dream'" printed on it rises above what looks like a landscape drawn in a child's formula for infinite hills. There is a crystal ball, a handle, and a spark. The numbers "2 3 8 10 7 1," and beneath that "3 2 5 4 1," appear mysteriously in the mechanism. Mileage perhaps, on a post Oz odometer, spun by geography.

Her line is direct and key to the sensibility in her art. Often pen-and-ink, and like watercolor not correctable, it is, as Robert Creeley has said of poetic line, "a locus of experience, not a presumption of expected value." Thus when James Merrill, in his praise of the painting *Merida from the Roof,* singles out "an absurd ornamental urn (so much for Art?)," he speaks as much of the affecting modesty of these pictures as of anything else. Seeing them, we are ultimately and charmingly disarmed, and left to look and look.

PAINTINGS

41 CHARLES STREET

[undated]

Watercolor, gouache, and ink

8 ¼ x 6 ¾ inches

Collection of Alice Methfessel

A candidate for Bishop's earliest-known painting. Ivy curls like smoke around the cat-eyed windows of a Greenwich Village house. In shifting shades of red, orange, and russet (set off by a blue garbage can) the picture is held together by a web of hatched and gridded lines. In 1934, Bishop lived at 16 Charles Street – a block away from number 41. Today a modern brownstone complex occupies the address.

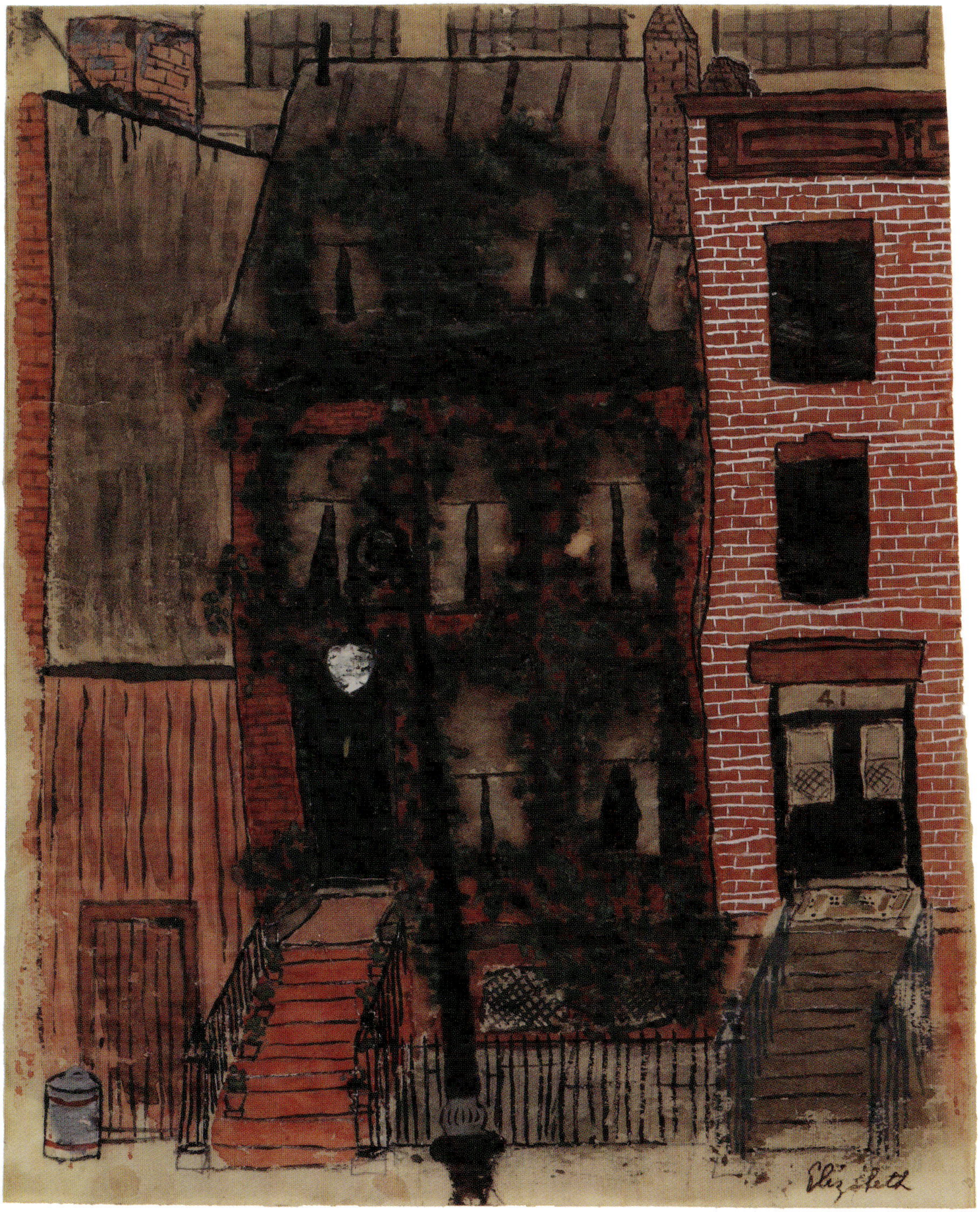
41
Elizabeth

SHA SHA

[1937]

watercolor

9 x 6 inches

Collection of Vassar College Library

Sha-Sha is the nickname of Charlotte Russell, a Florida friend of Bishop's. Above the wainscoting panels whose wood grain complete with mildew receives special attention, a simple mathematical equation is written on the wall: "1 + 4 = 7." As perhaps a comment on other "inaccuracies" in the picture – the anatomy of the figure, the invisible chair she sits on – it boasts, like them, a pictorial rightness of its own.

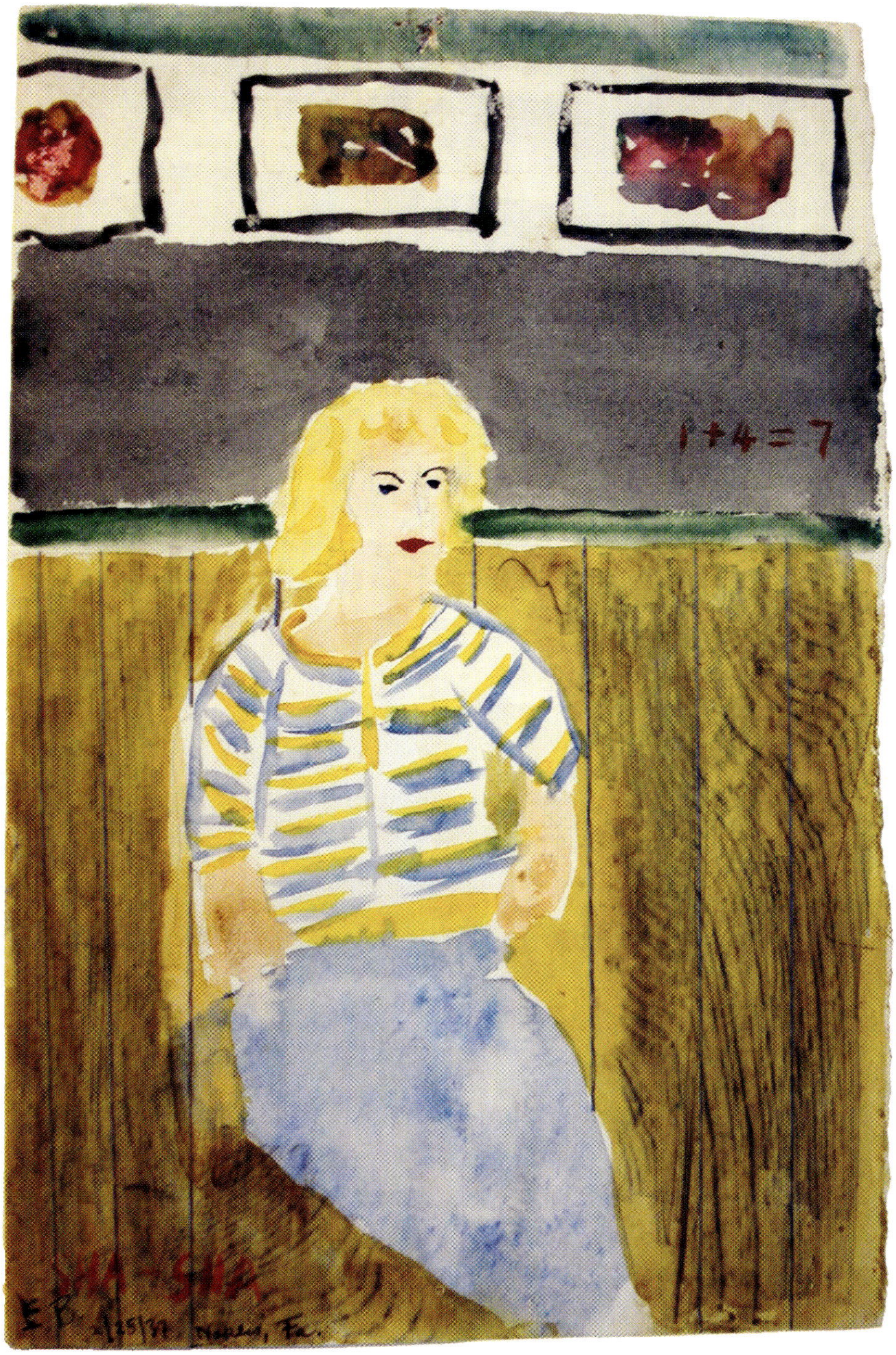
1+4=7
SHA-SHA
E.B.

MURRAY HILL HOTEL

[*undated*]

pencil

6 ½ x 5 ¼ inches

Collection of Vassar College Library

The emptiness of the chair and the act of drawing it evoke, in the mood of an Edward Hopper, nights spent alone in a New York hotel. Bishop stayed at the Murray Hill a number of times in the late thirties and early forties.

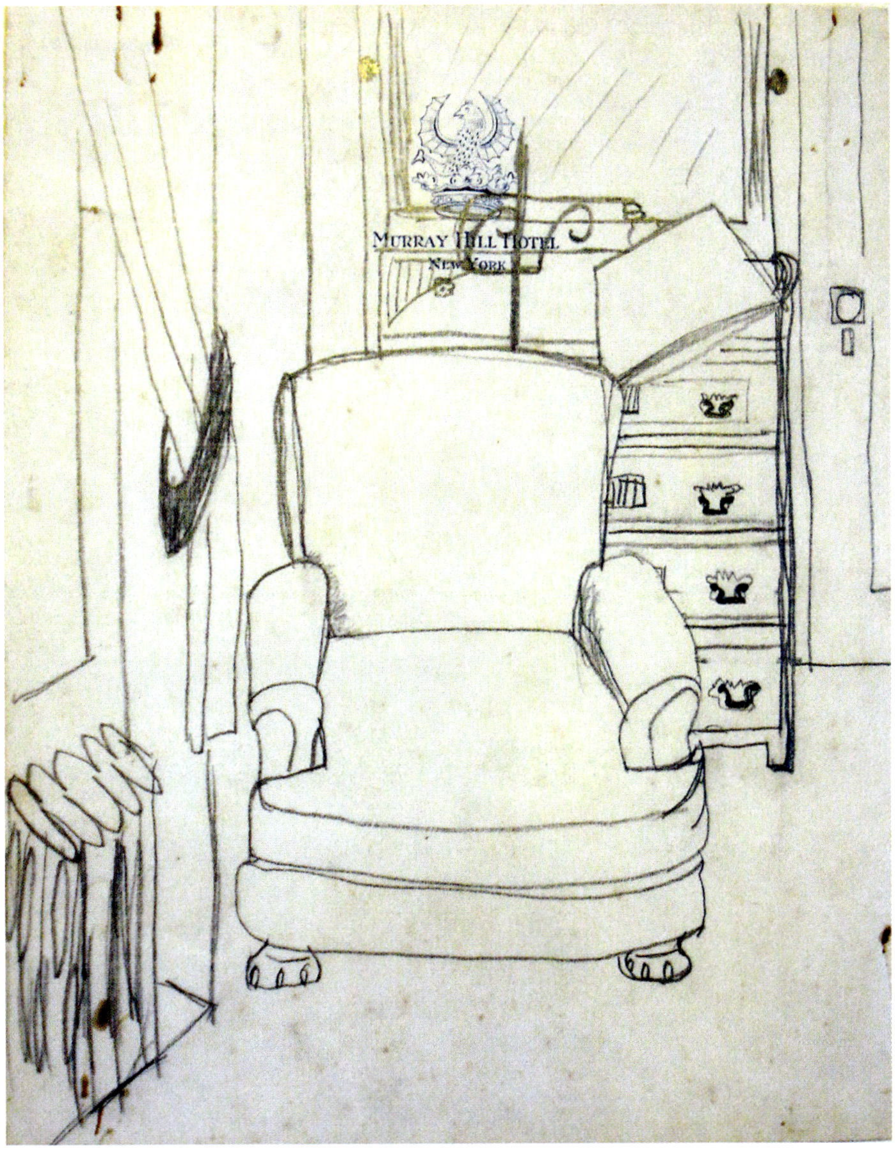
MURRAY HILL HOTEL
NEW YORK

PALAIS DU SENAT

[1938]

watercolor and gouache

5 ½ x 9 inches

Collection of Dorothee Bowie

Henry Miller (a fellow watercolorist) wrote ecstatically about his discovery of Chinese white. Bishop uses it here in a way that turns the architecture of her line into a painterly strength.

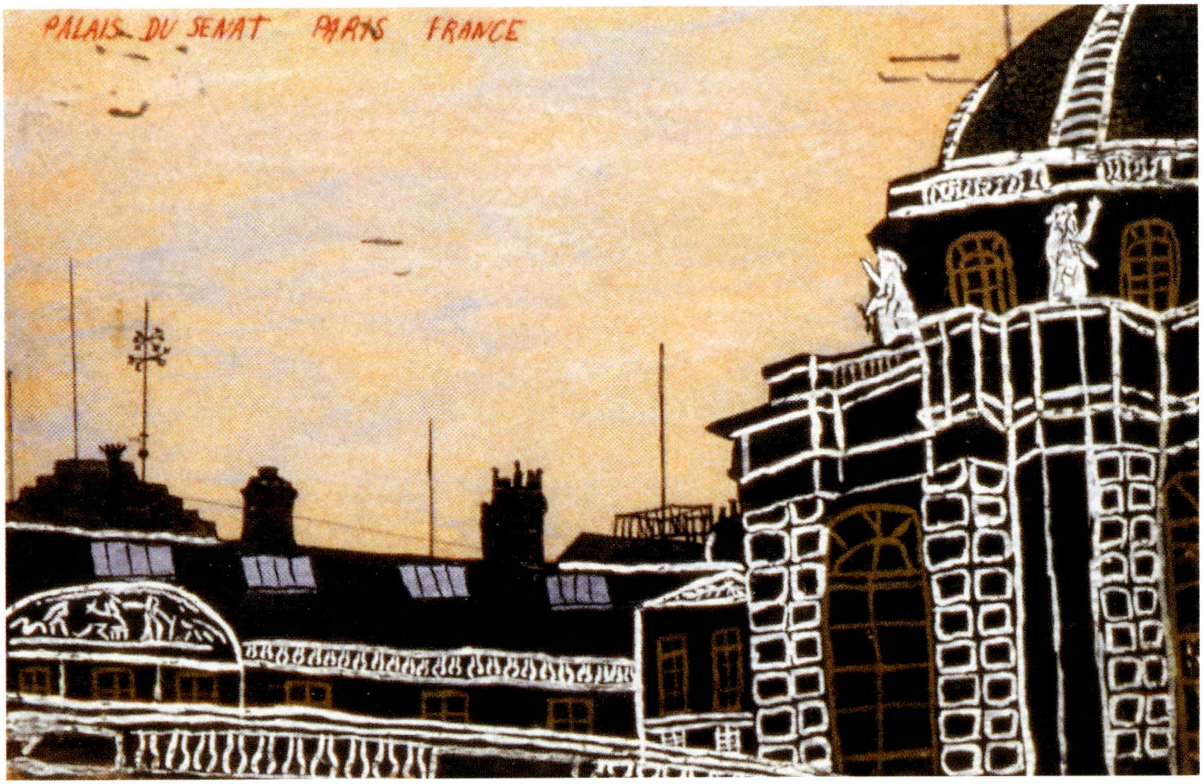
PALAIS DU SENAT PARIS FRANCE

SLEEPING FIGURE

[undated]

watercolor and gouache

8 ½ x 5 ½ inches

Collection of Alice Methfessel

The doll-like figure is almost certainly Louise Crane. Bishop traveled with her in Europe, and they lived together in Key West.

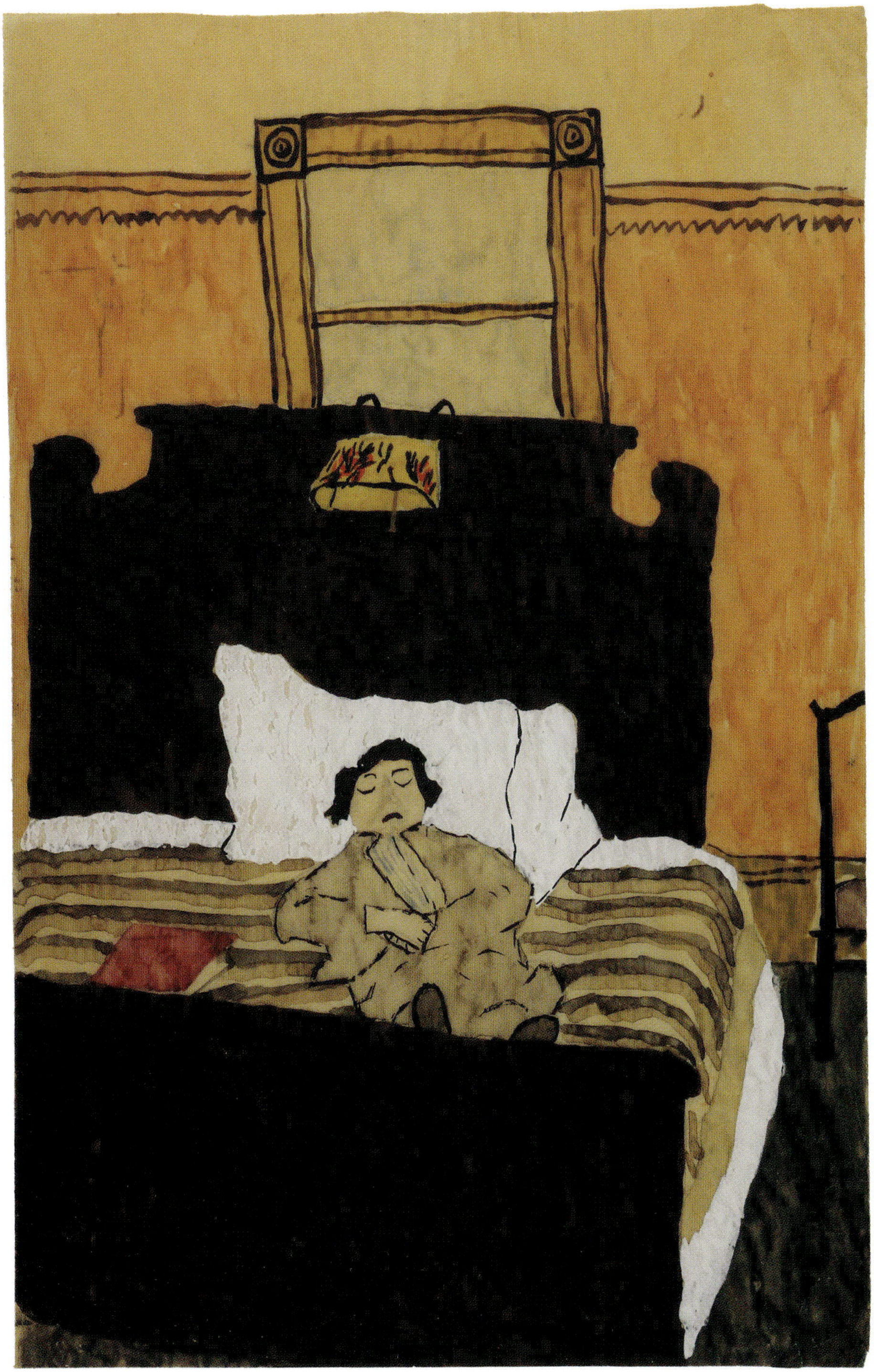

FIREPLACE

[undated]

ink and watercolor

3 x 3 inches

Collection of Vassar College Library

This tiny, energetic mix of thick and thin lines with the pale wash of a glowing fire is like an illustration for a story. On the mantle, Bishop has drawn: a shark, two burning candles, and a clock with a black heart for a face.

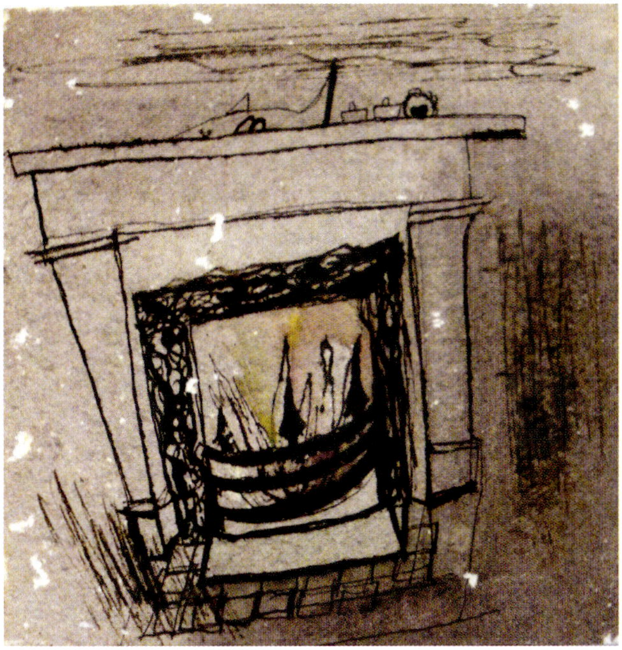

TABLE WITH PLAID CLOTH

[*undated*]

watercolor and gouache

7 ½ x 5 ¾ inches

Collection of Vassar College Library

Vellum, which allowed pigments to sit unabsorbed on the surface of a sheet, was used to enhance the intensity of watercolor. Unfortunately, the papers become brittle with age. The framed painting on the table, propped against the wall, is possibly a Calder.

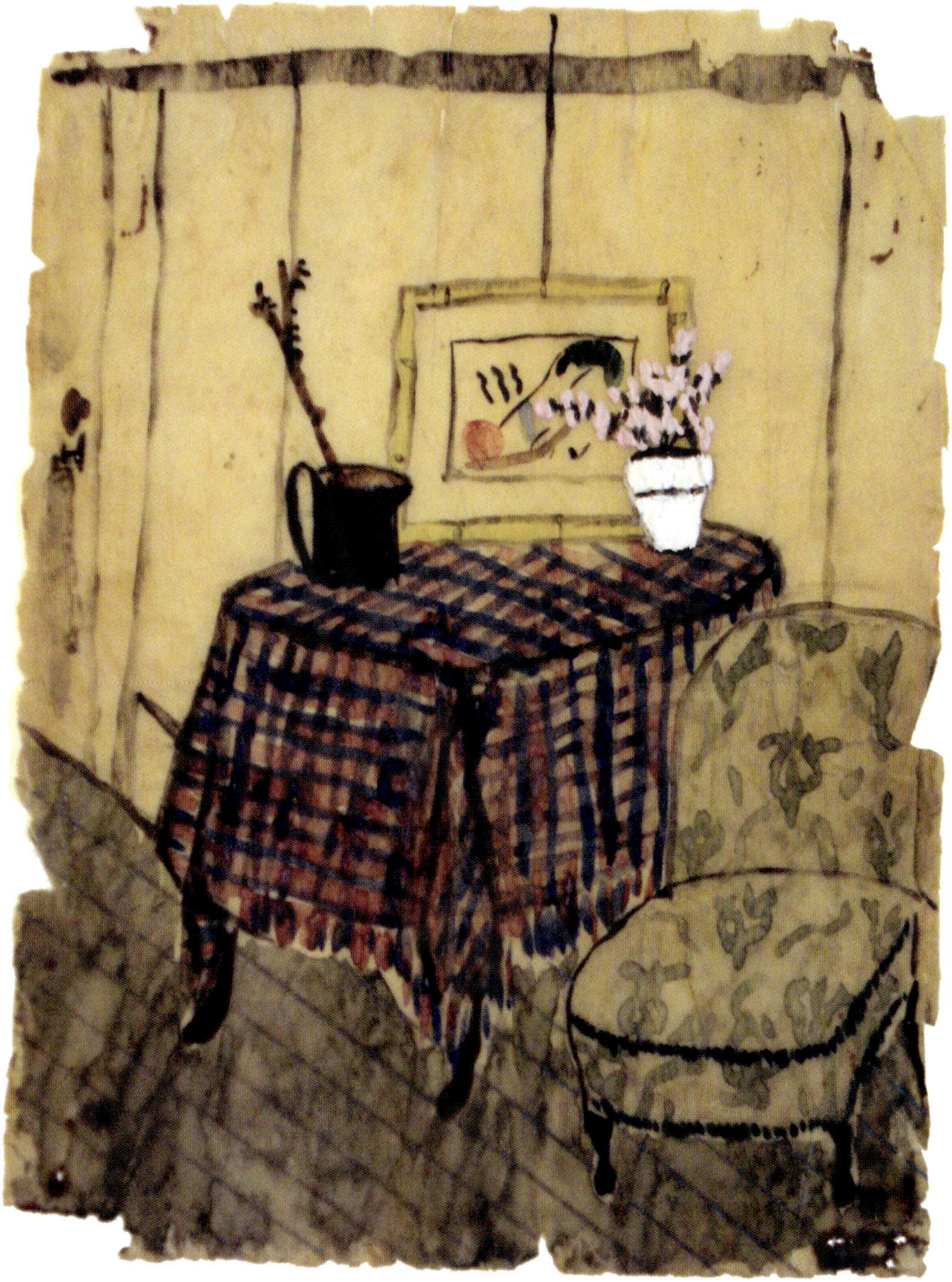

NOVA SCOTIA LANDSCAPE

[undated]

watercolor and gouache

5 ¼ x 8 inches

Collection of Frani Blough Muser

The small multicolored strokes that depict the lake raise to a level of formal invention the entire foreground of a simple rural scene. Bishop has a feel for the task-like execution of patterns and their abstract elements.

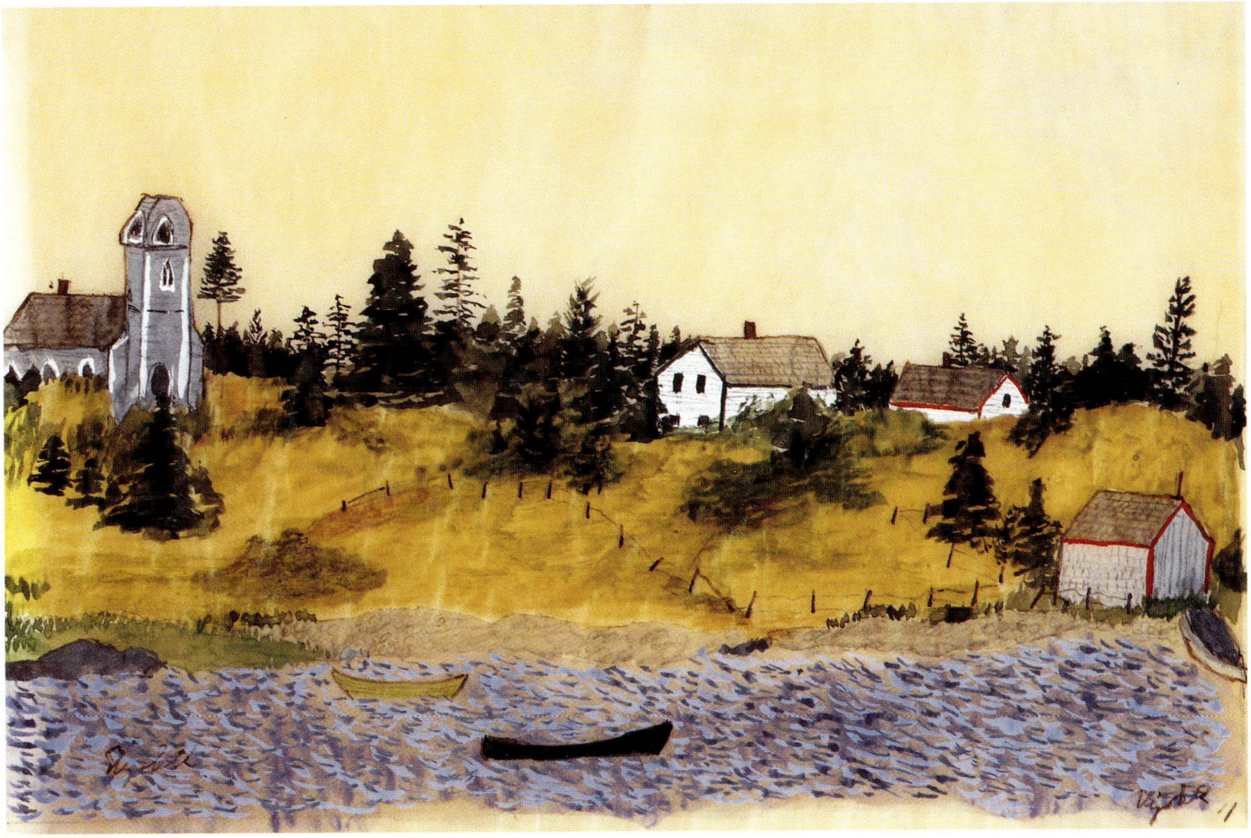

OLIVIA

[undated]

watercolor and gouache

5 x 7 inches

Collection of Alice Methfessel

A church of weathered wood on Olivia Street in Key West. Bishop adds a tilted steeple made of power lines and "heaven."

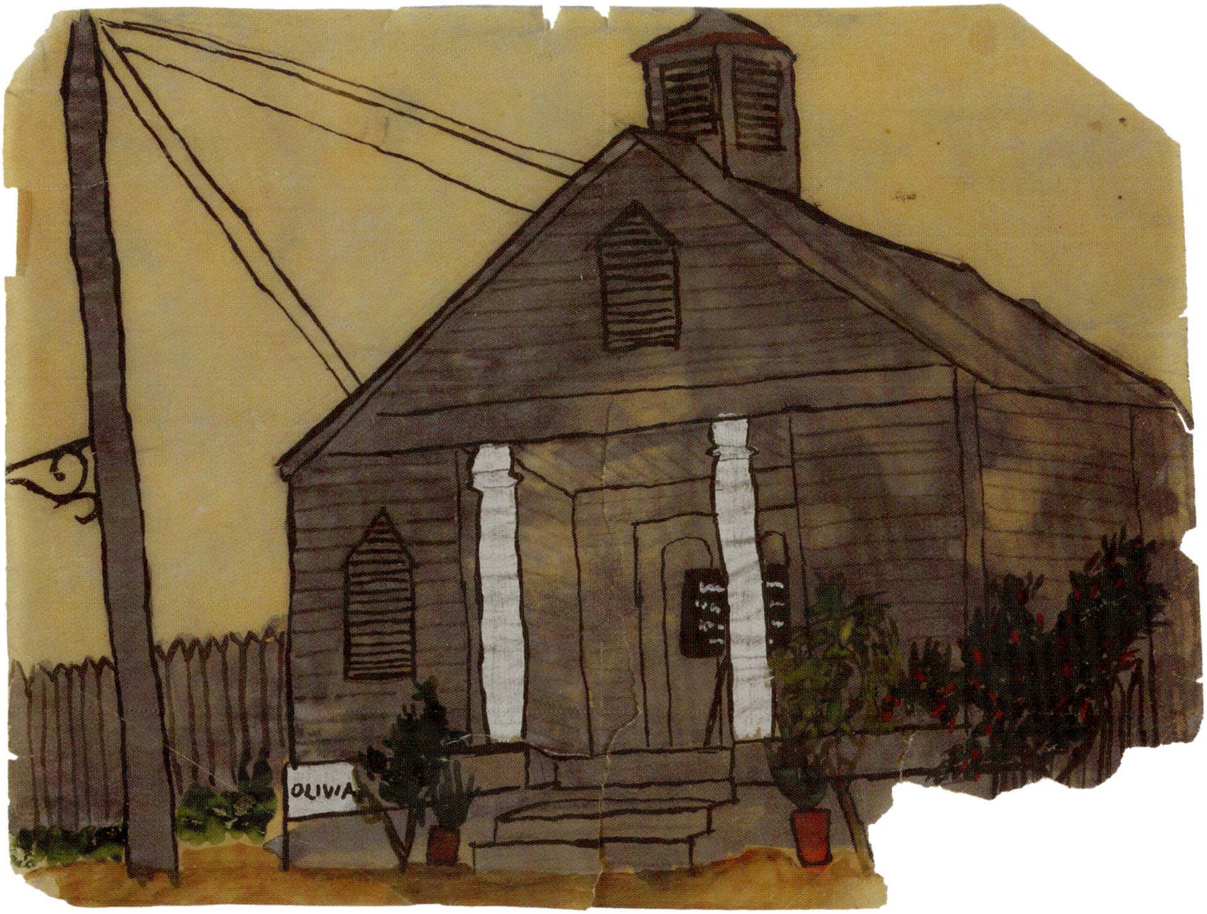
OLIVIA

HARRIS SCHOOL

[undated]

watercolor, gouache, and ink

10 ½ x 9 ½ inches

Private Collection, courtesy Alexandre Gallery, New York; Photo: Takenori Nishijima

Against the weighty symmetry of this Key West picture, Bishop rhymes the bicycle with the two circular planters. The kites, themselves slant rhymes, surmount the rigid façade of the building, their tails dancing in the sky. Yet they too are tethered to the earth by visible strings. The painting is an overt "idea of order." Harris School is still there today, although the trees and flower beds have given way to a wider street.

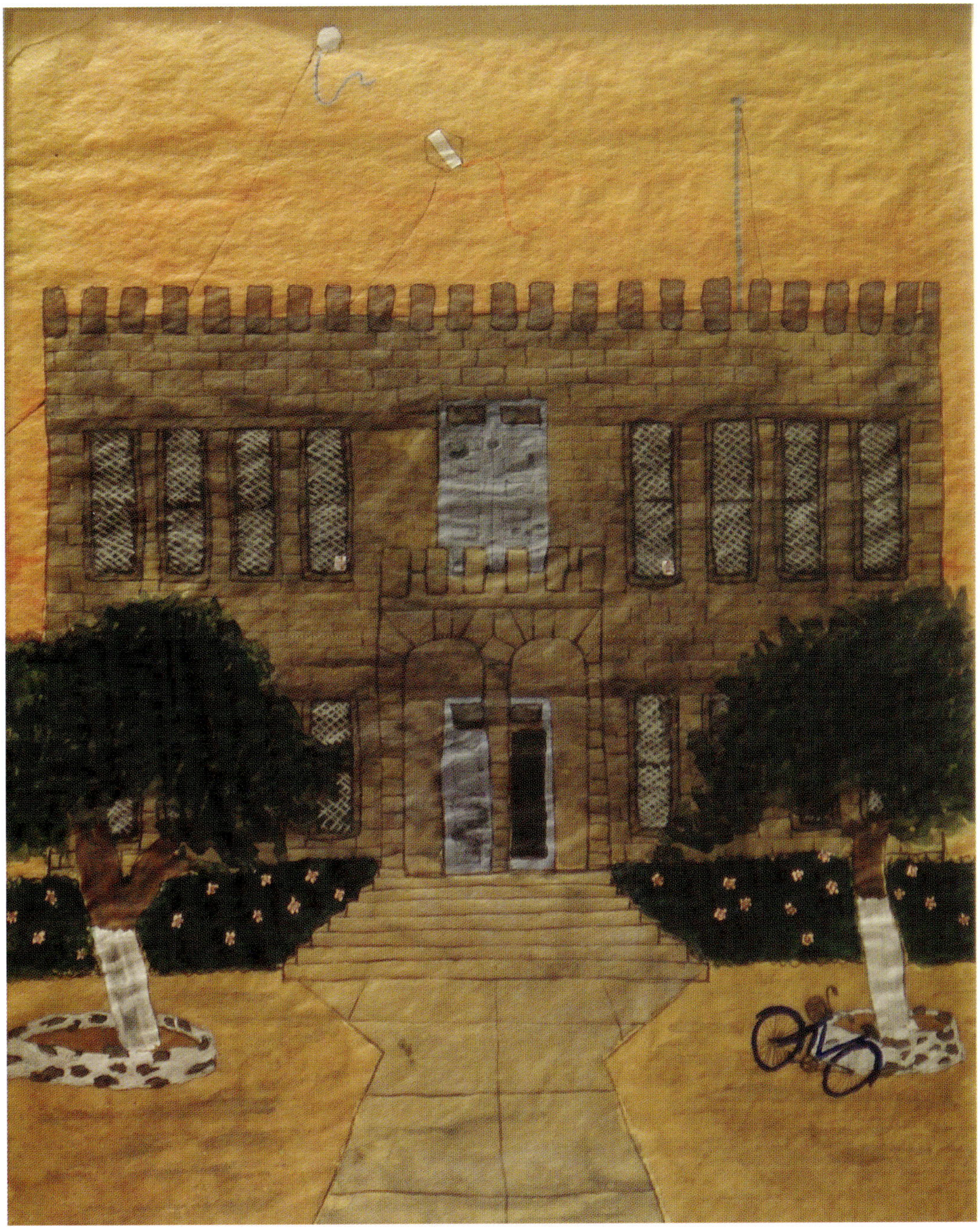

COUNTY COURTHOUSE

[undated]

watercolor, gouache, and ink

5 ½ x 6 inches

Collection of Alice Methfessel

A view composed of what obstructs it. The central triangle that leads the eye into the painting is at once overwhelmed by foliage. Downed power lines contribute to the sense of disorder. The scene is the exact opposite of what a Sunday watercolorist might select. It is, in fact, a picture whose wit transforms it from a "scene" into an image of impasse.

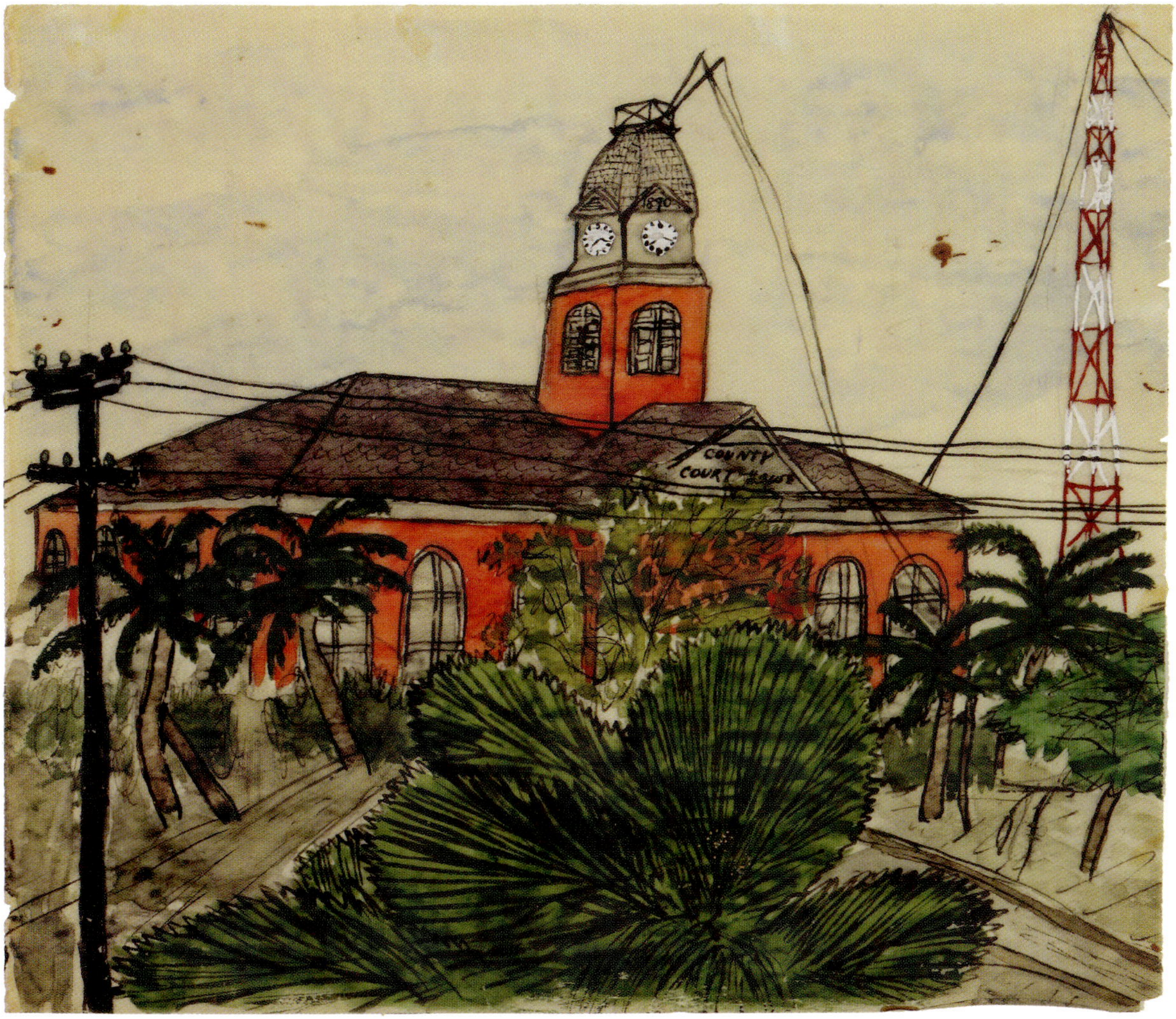
1890
COUNTY
COURT

THE ARMORY, KEY WEST

[undated]

watercolor. gouache, and ink

12 x 9 inches

Collection of Margaret Miller

The Key West Armory is on White Street, not far from the house at 624 – now a national literary landmark – where Bishop lived from 1938 to 1941.

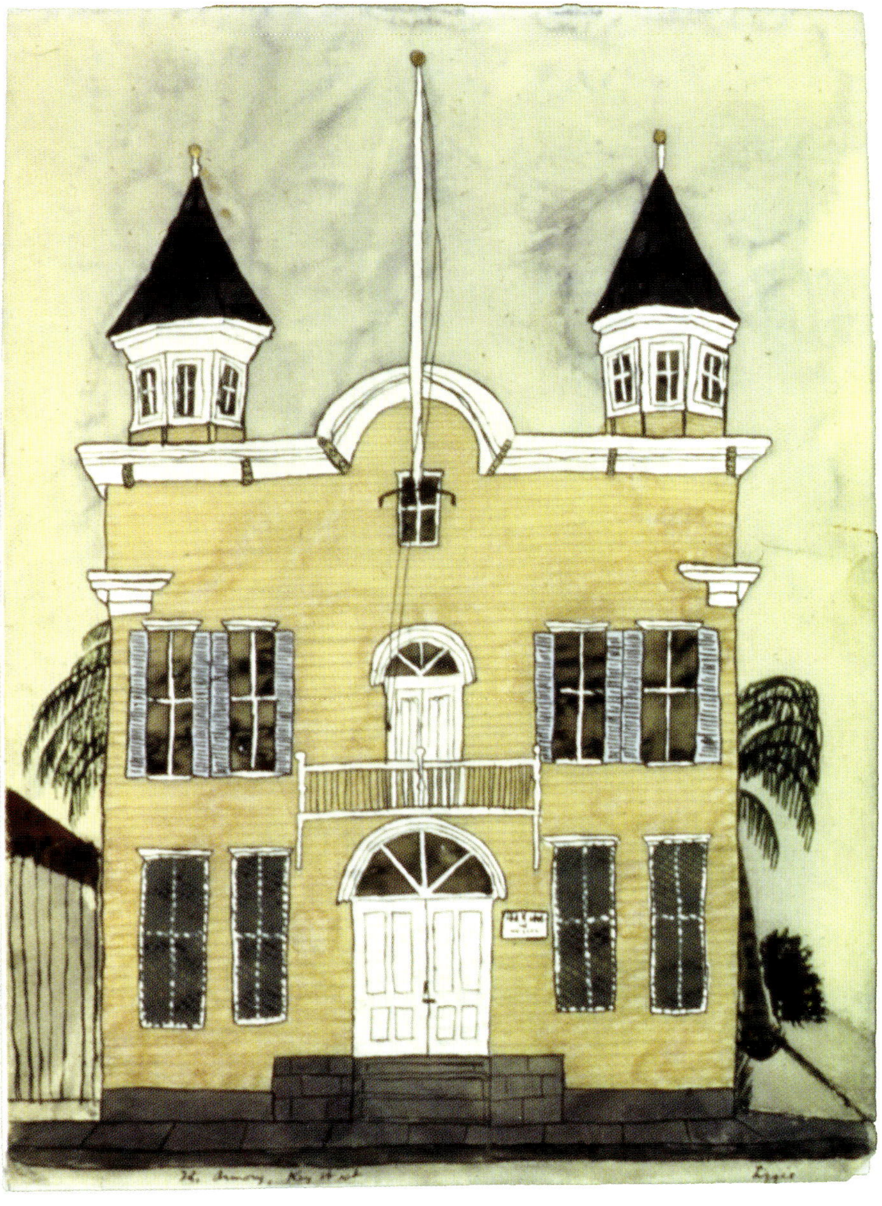

MERIDA FROM THE ROOF

[1942]

8 ½ x 11 ½ inches

Collection of Alice Methfessel

Bishop traveled in Mexico in the spring of 1942 with Marjorie Stevens. "Oaxaca is very nice – I like it next best to Merida, I think," she wrote to Marianne Moore. This picture, the jacket illustration for the original edition of *The Complete Poems: 1927-1979,* fans out from the tall palm at the edge of a hotel balcony with the verve and deftness of a David Hockney (who was five the year it was painted). Spots of random color play over the surface like pure abstraction, pinning down the busy composition of steeples, windmills, and palm trees as gulls wheel dramatically in a windy sky.

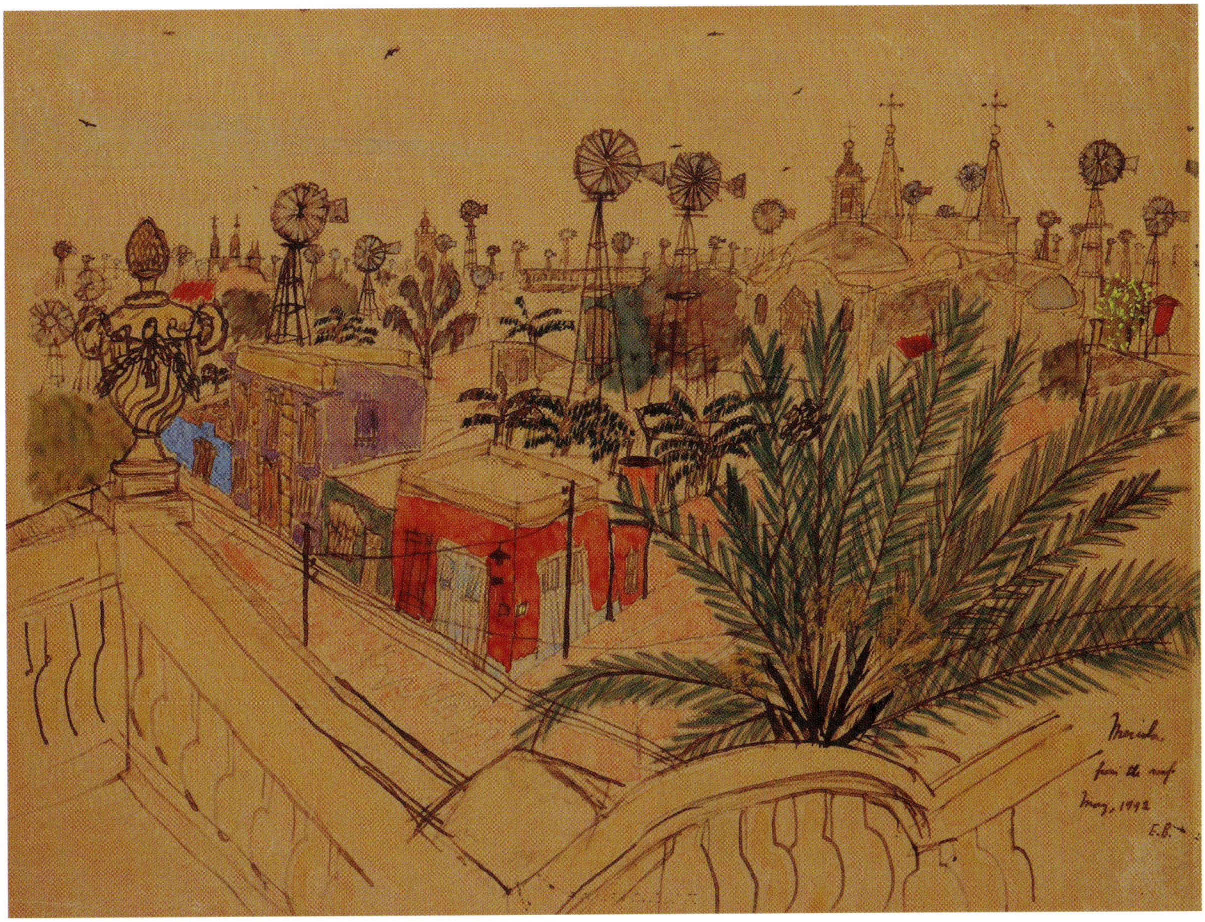
Merida.
from the roof
May, 1942
E.B.

GRAVE WITH FLORAL WREATHS

[undated]

watercolor and gouache

6 x 6 ½ inches

Collection of Vassar College Library

This cemetery, with its raised graves and "decorations," is a landmark in Key West.

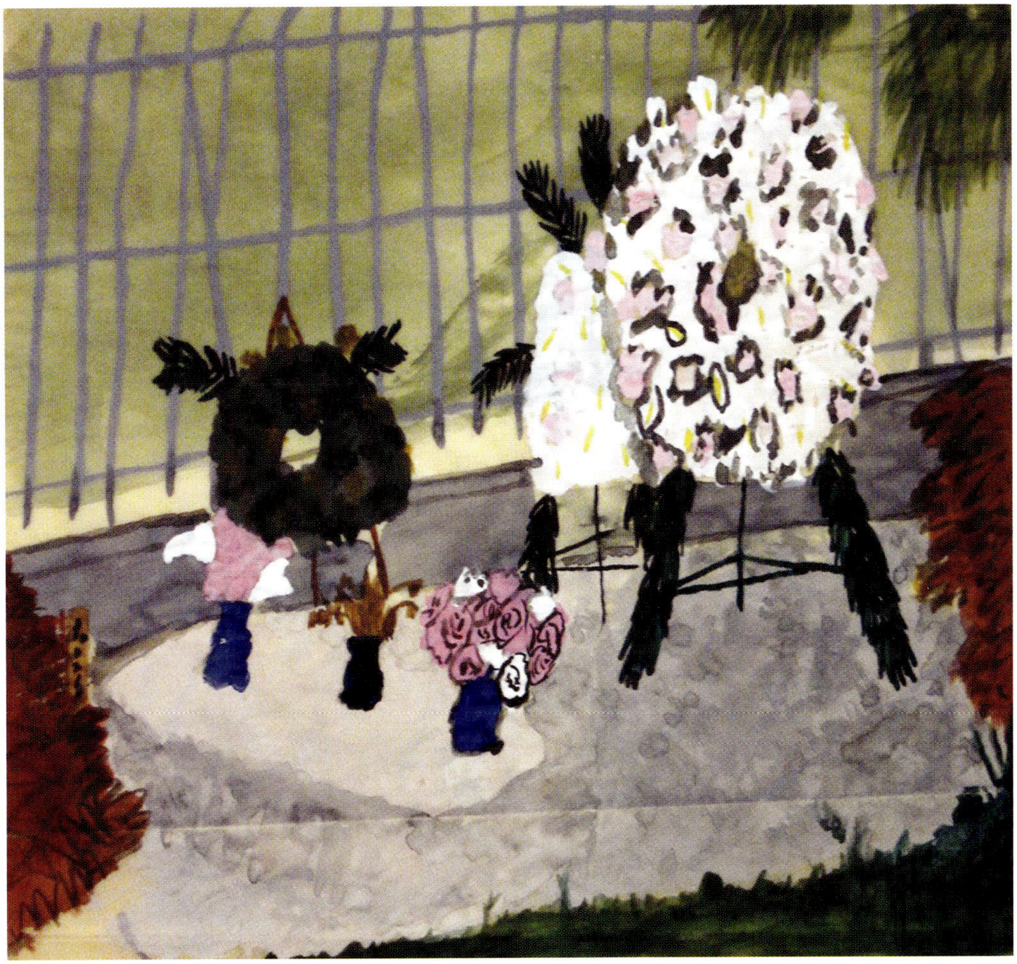

TOMBSTONES FOR SALE

[undated]

watercolor, gouache, and ink

6 x 9 inches

Collection of Alice Methfessel

The jacket illustration for the original edition of *The Collected Prose.* Composed out of many of the same elements as the early "41 Charles Street," its wit and calm insouciance show the fluent maturity of her best Key West pictures. The blossoming poinciana tree floats gracefully over the business of life and death. Beneath it, the neon blue of a flower box has the value of a perfectly placed period.

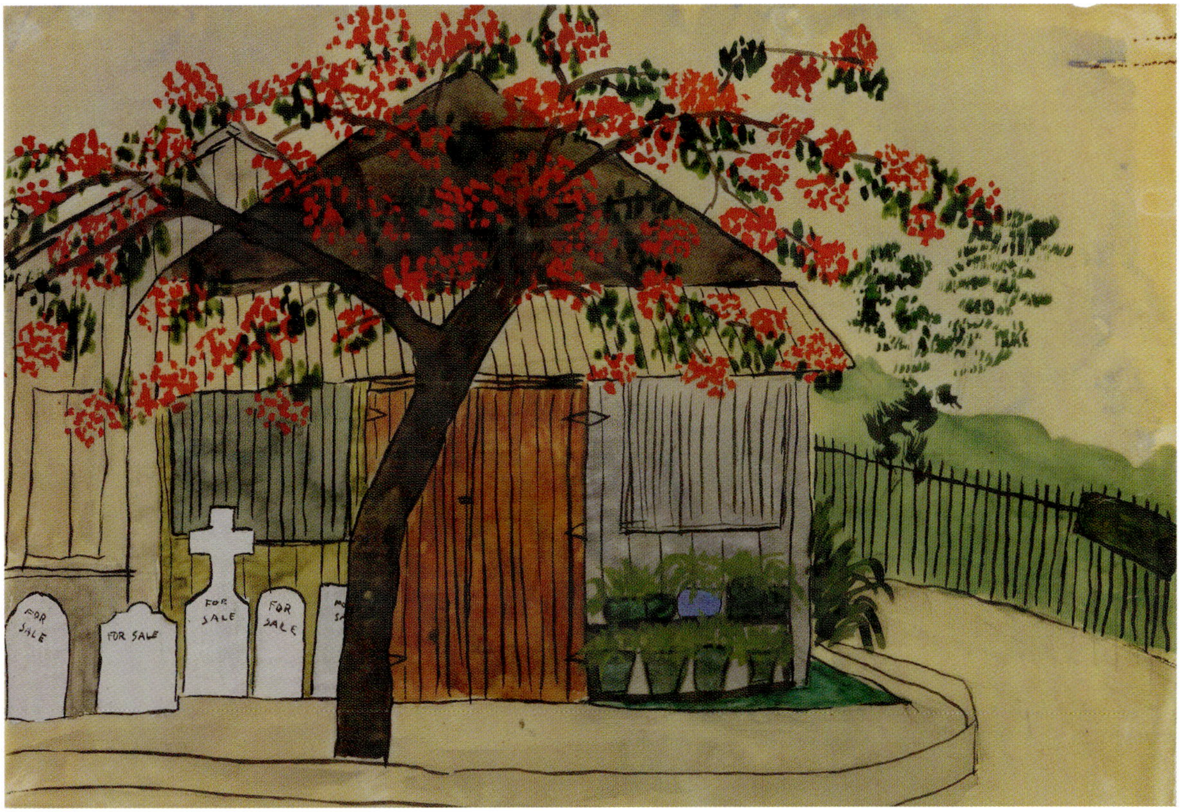
FOR SALE
FOR SALE
FOR SALE
FOR SALE

GRAVEYARD WITH FENCED GRAVES

[undated]

Watercolor and gouache

5 ¾ x 6 ¾ inches

Collection of Vassar College Library

This could be a pendant to *Tombstones for Sale*; the poinciana tree – this time in the Key West cemetery – shades several tombstones that have "sold."

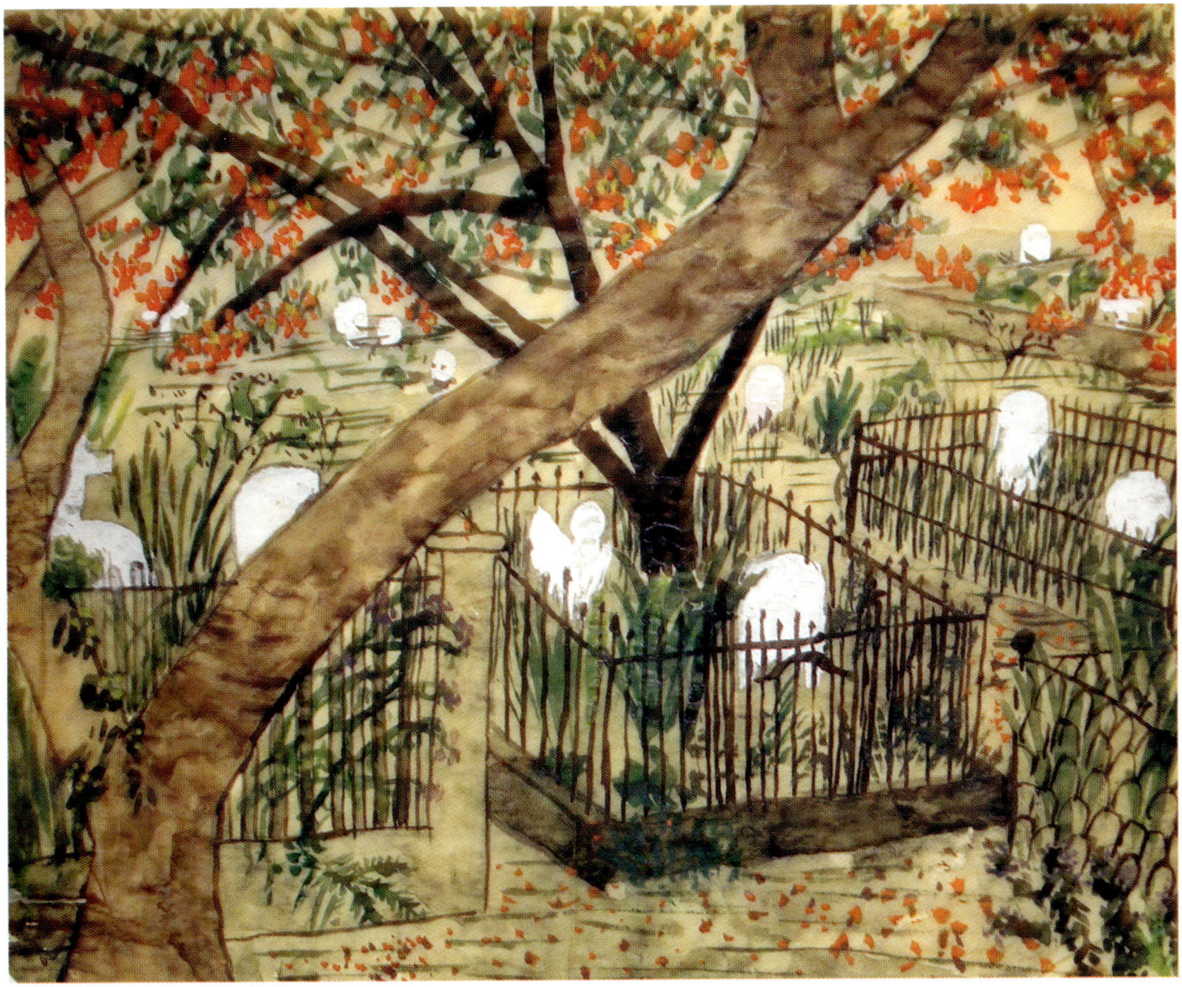

BEGONIAS AND COLEUS

[undated]

pastel

6 ⅛ x 9 ⅛ inches

Collection of Vassar College Library

The flowers and leaves are accurately drawn with a sureness of hand, while on the fence behind them sketchy marks of lavender vie with petals of the same hue, in a contrast that is both subtle and lively.

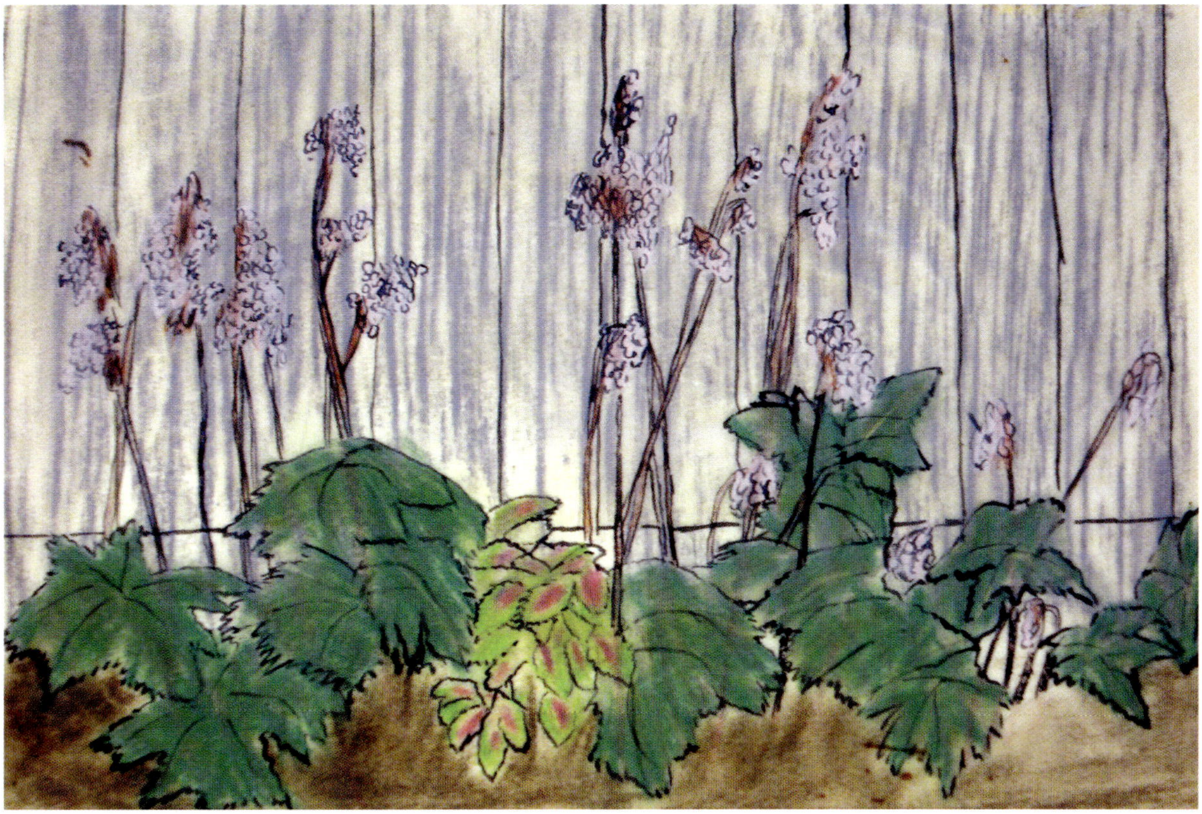

STAR CACTUS

[undated]

watercolor and ink

5 ¾ x 6 inches

Collection of Vassar College Library

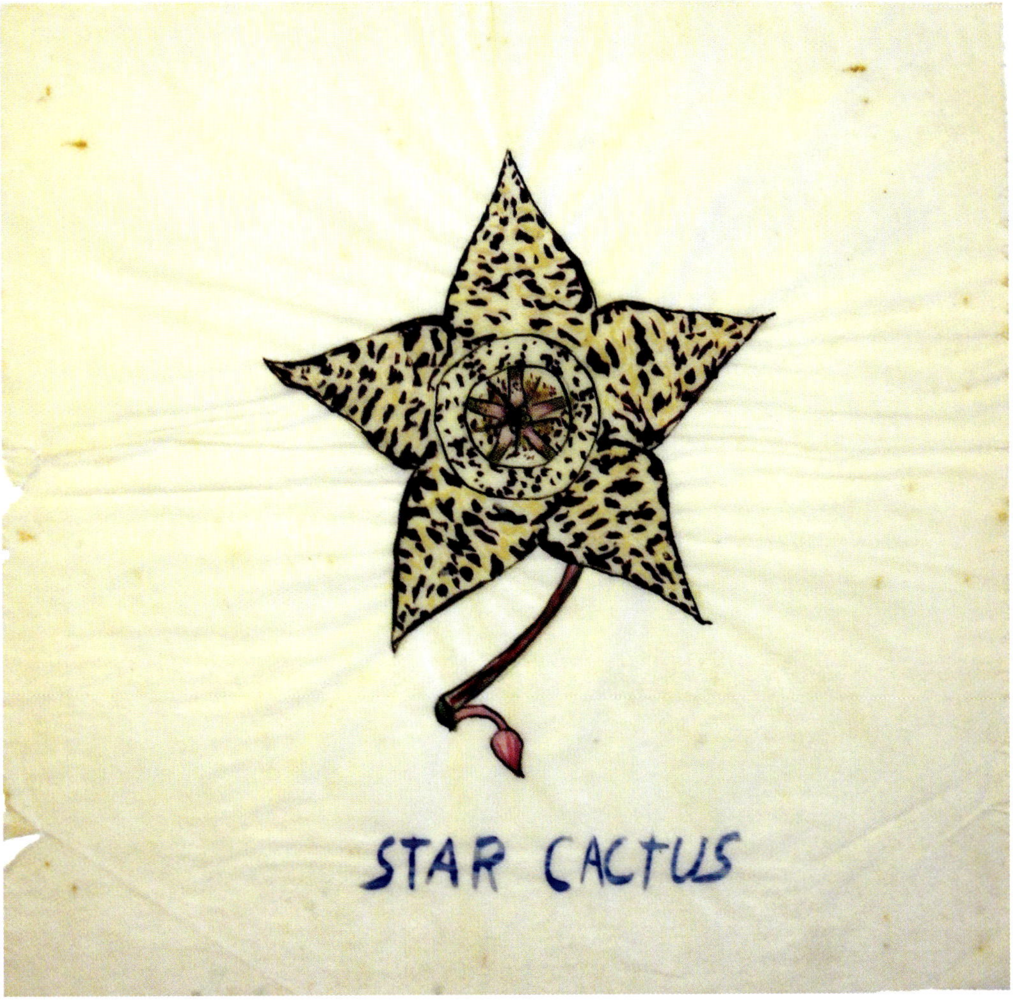
STAR CACTUS

CROTON

[undated]

watercolor

9 x 5 ¾ inches

Collection of Vassar College Library

This vividly colored croton leaf and the preceding star cactus, both painted as single images and named on the sheet, suggest that Bishop may have begun a series of botanical studies.

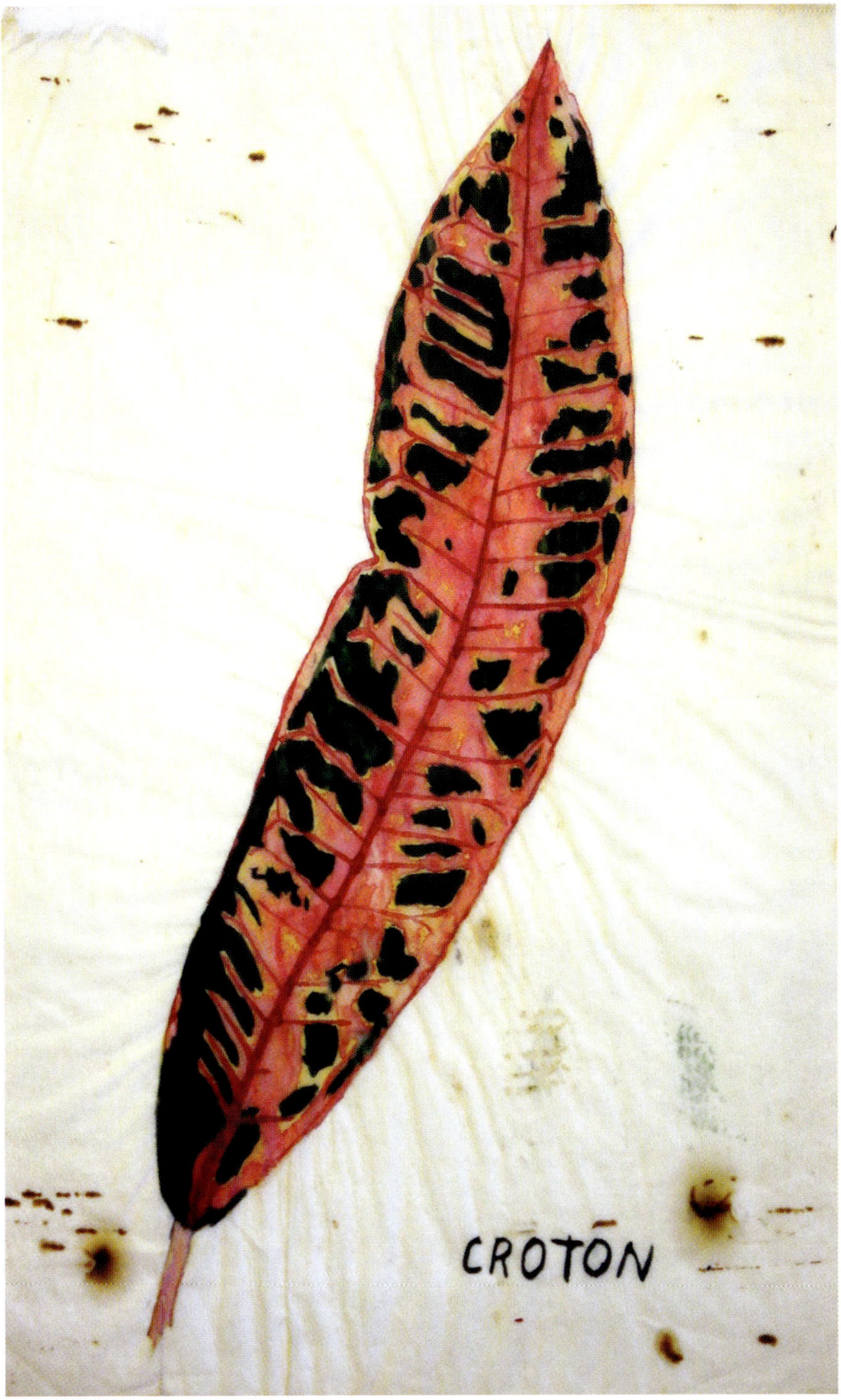
CROTON

DAISIES IN PAINT BUCKET

[undated]

watercolor and gouache

10 ½ x 9 ½ inches

Private Collection, courtesy Alexandre Gallery, New York; Photo: Takenori Nishijima

Used as the jacket illustration for *One Art: Letters.* The paint bucket full of flowers sits dead center in the composition and as far front as possible. It has the aplomb of a masterpiece. Gray washes convey the shine of the paint bucket as well as a band of glue residue from a peeled-off label.

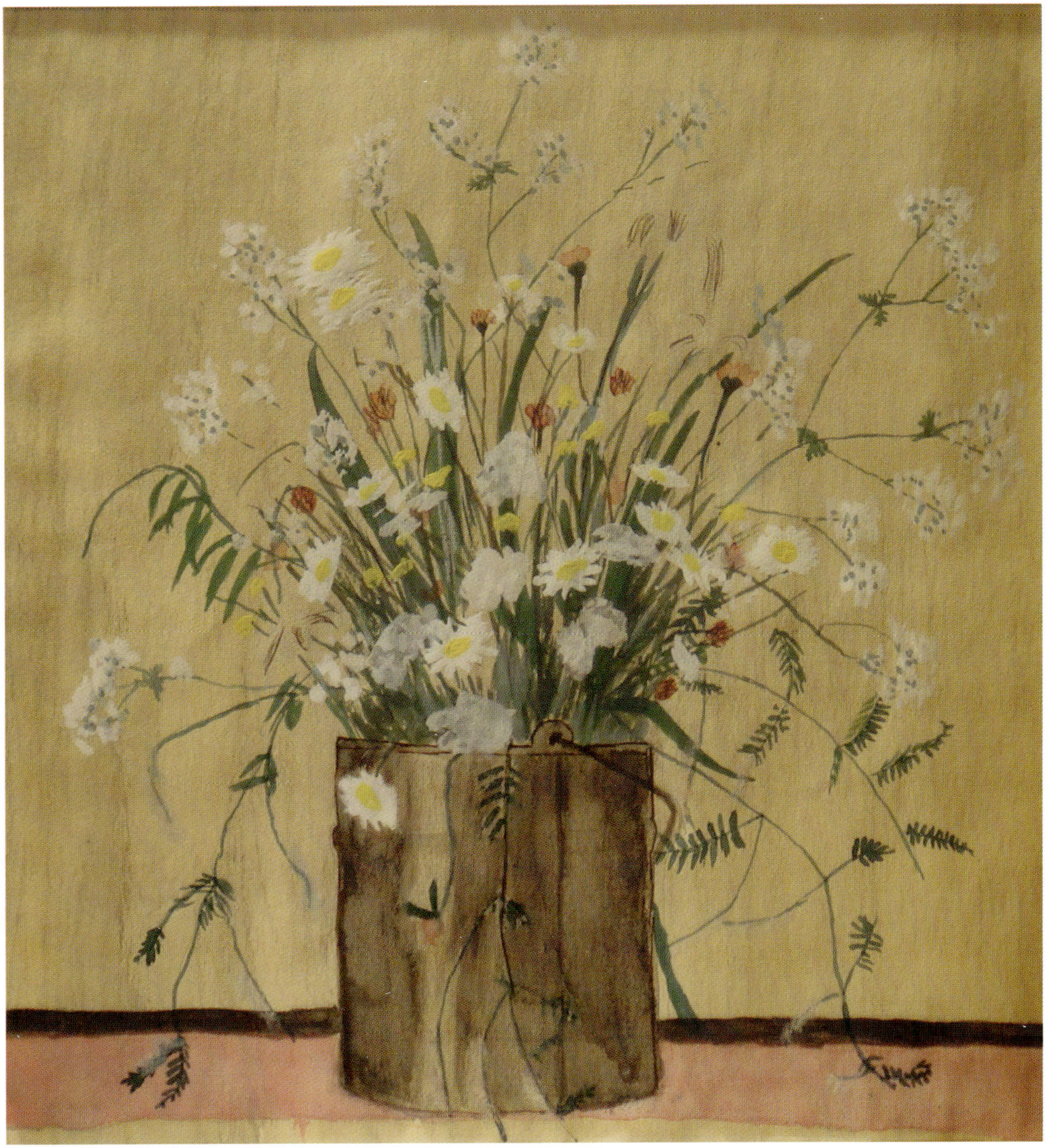

INTERIOR WITH EXTENSION CORD

[undated]

watercolor, gouache, and ink

6 ⅛ x 6 ⅛ inches

Private Collection, courtesy Alexandre Gallery, New York; Photo: Takenori Nishijima

The general rule of a Bishop picture is: if a table exists, put flowers on it. In this case, with the dramatic focus on the extension cord crossing the planes of the white room (to bring a lamp to the narrow working space), she simply opened the door to the garden instead.

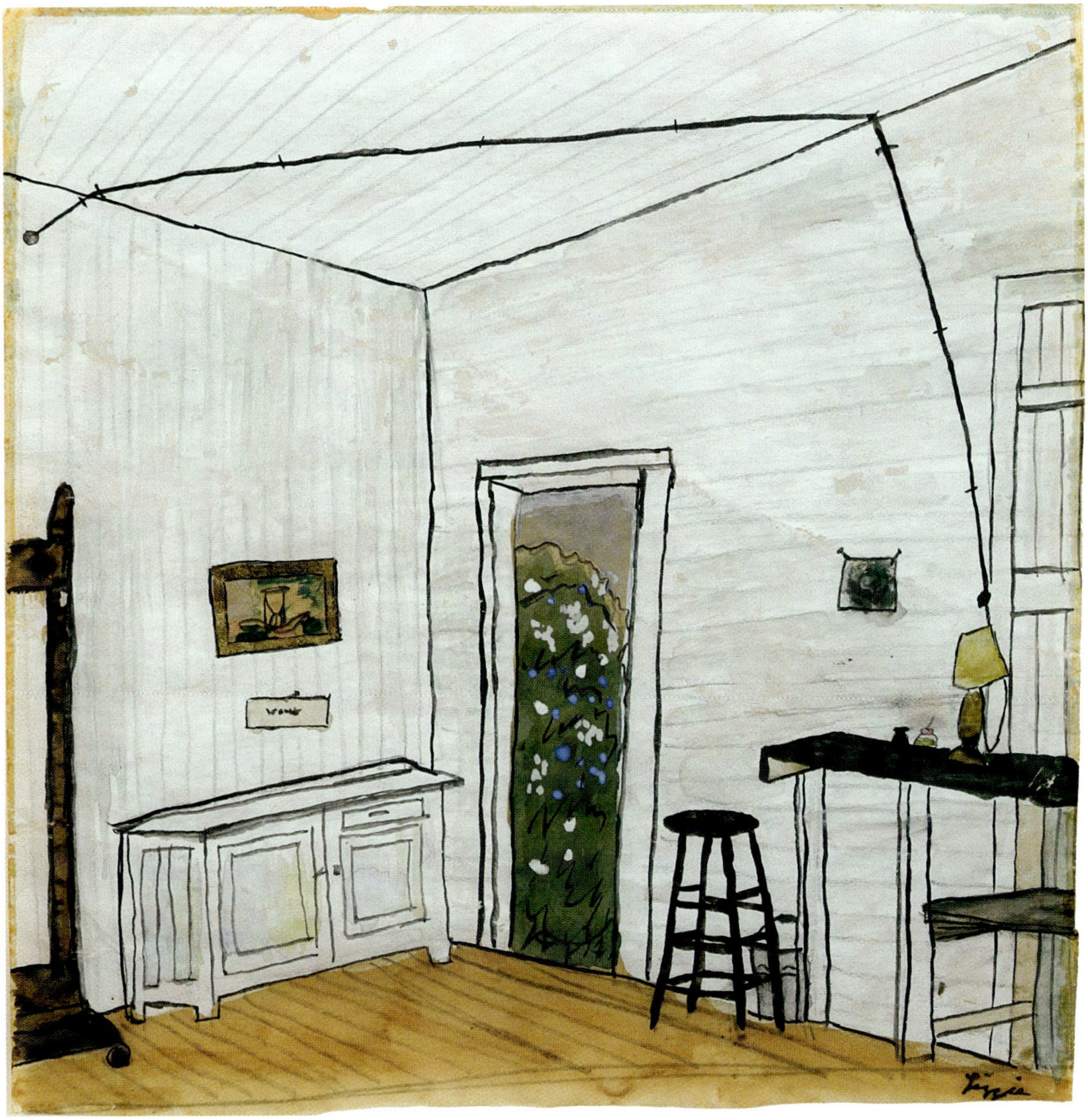

CABIN WITH PORTHOLE

[*undated*]

watercolor and gouache

whereabouts unknown

Books, bags, manuscripts loaded on board, this has the *mise-en-scène* of a single frame in *The Adventures of Elizabeth Bishop.* One can almost envision an Hergé-like figure of the poet herself, propped up on the second bunk with her unpacked paints.

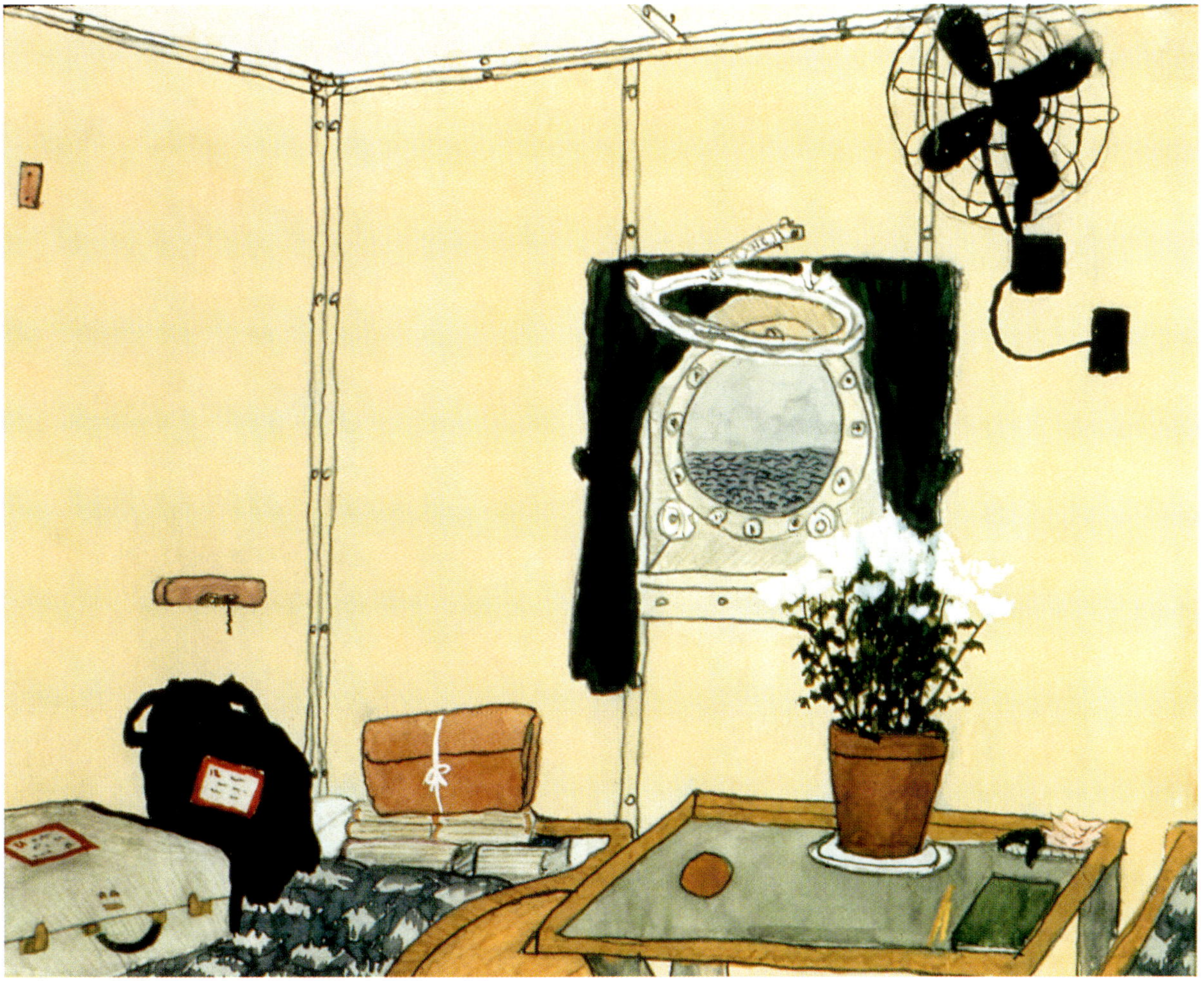

GRAY CHURCH

[undated]

watercolor

whereabouts unknown

Possibly the Brazilian town of Ouro Prêto, where Bishop owned Casa Mariana, the house she named after Marianne Moore. The church, viewed from a height that looks across to its patched roof, has an animation reminiscent of the paintings of Charles Burchfield.

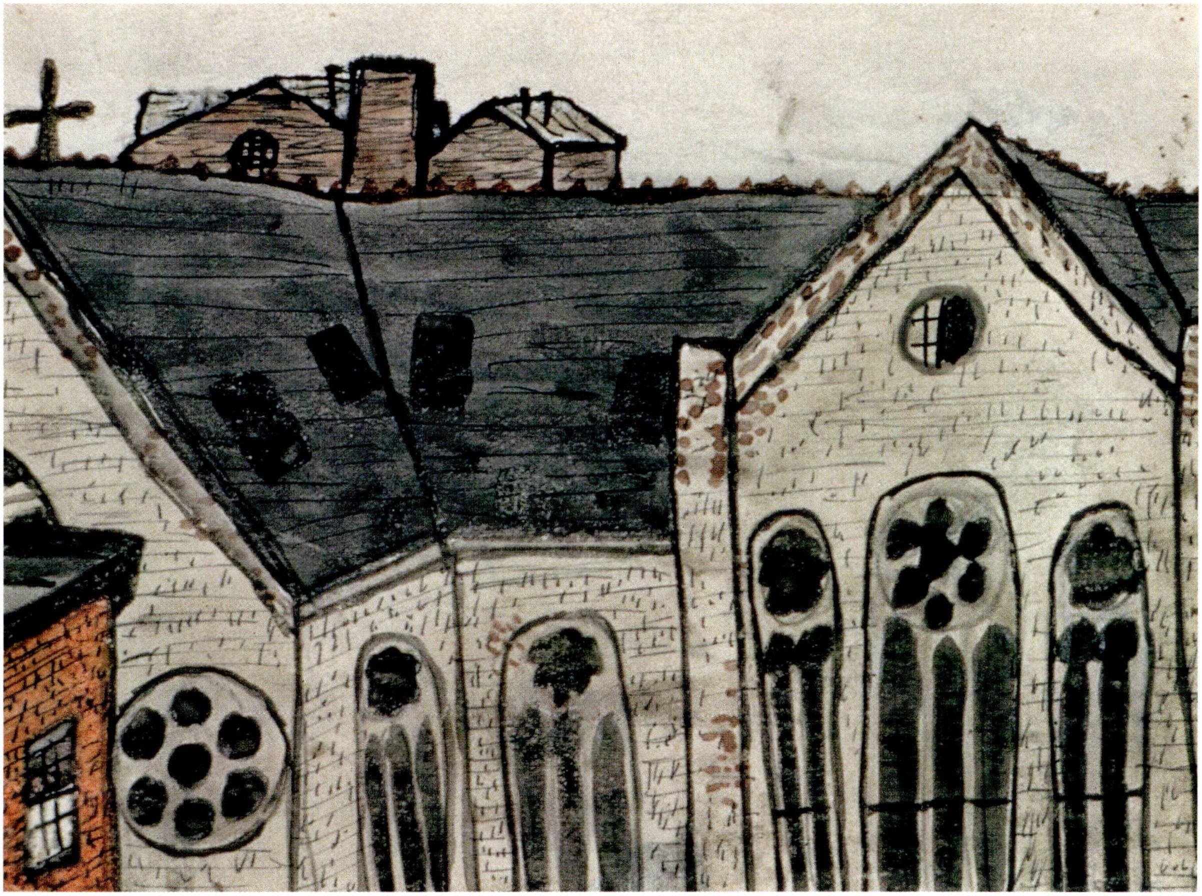

FEATHER BOX

[undated]

construction

10 x 17 x 3 inches

Collection of Alice Methfessel

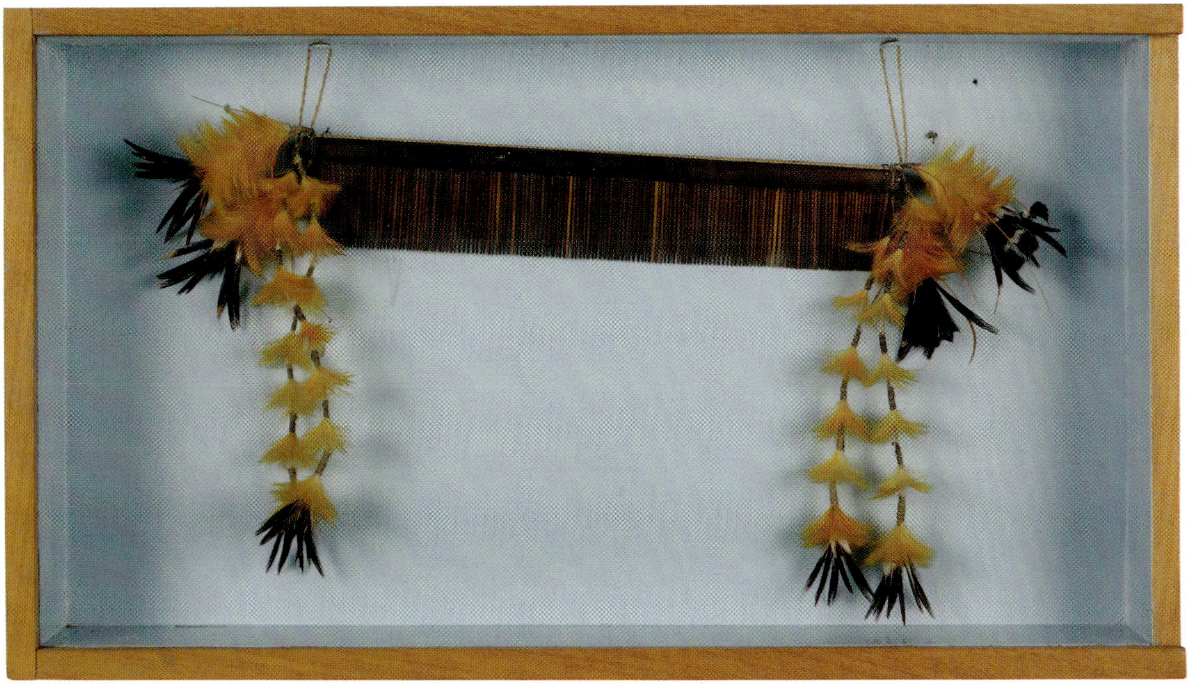

ANJINHOS

[undated]

collage construction

12 x 15 ½ x 2 inches

Collection of Alice Methfessel

Anjinhos (angels) was inspired by the drowning of a young girl in Rio de Janeiro. Both it and, to a lesser extent, *Feather Box* recall the work of Joseph Cornell – his "monuments to every moment," as Bishop translates the phrase in her version of Octavio Paz's poem "Objects & Apparitions," dedicated to Cornell.

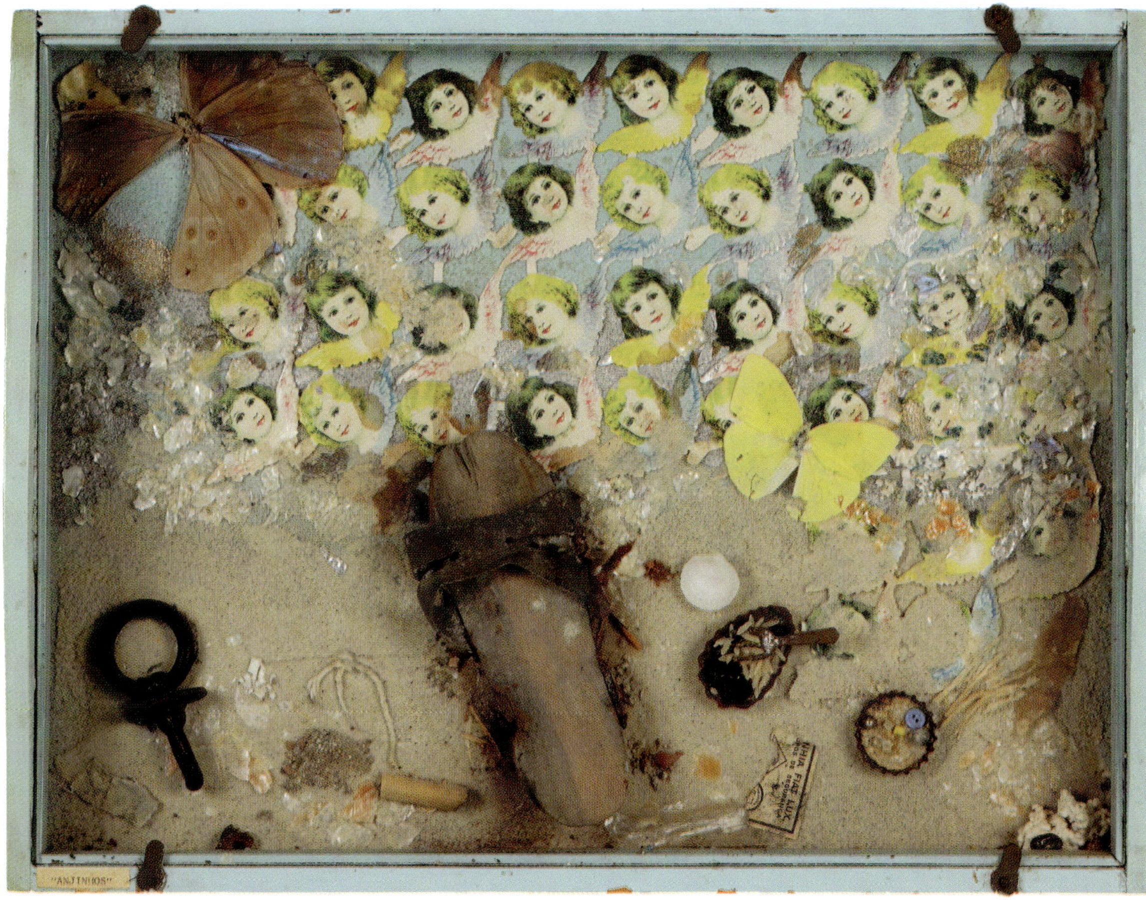
"ANJINHOS"

CHANDELIER

[undated]

watercolor and gouache

5 ⅝ x 8 ⅞ inches

Collection of Vassar College Library

This picture of a chandelier casting a multiple shadow on the ceiling was described by James Fenton as "surely another view from the bed, in one of those New York hotels in which Bishop spent many miserable months."

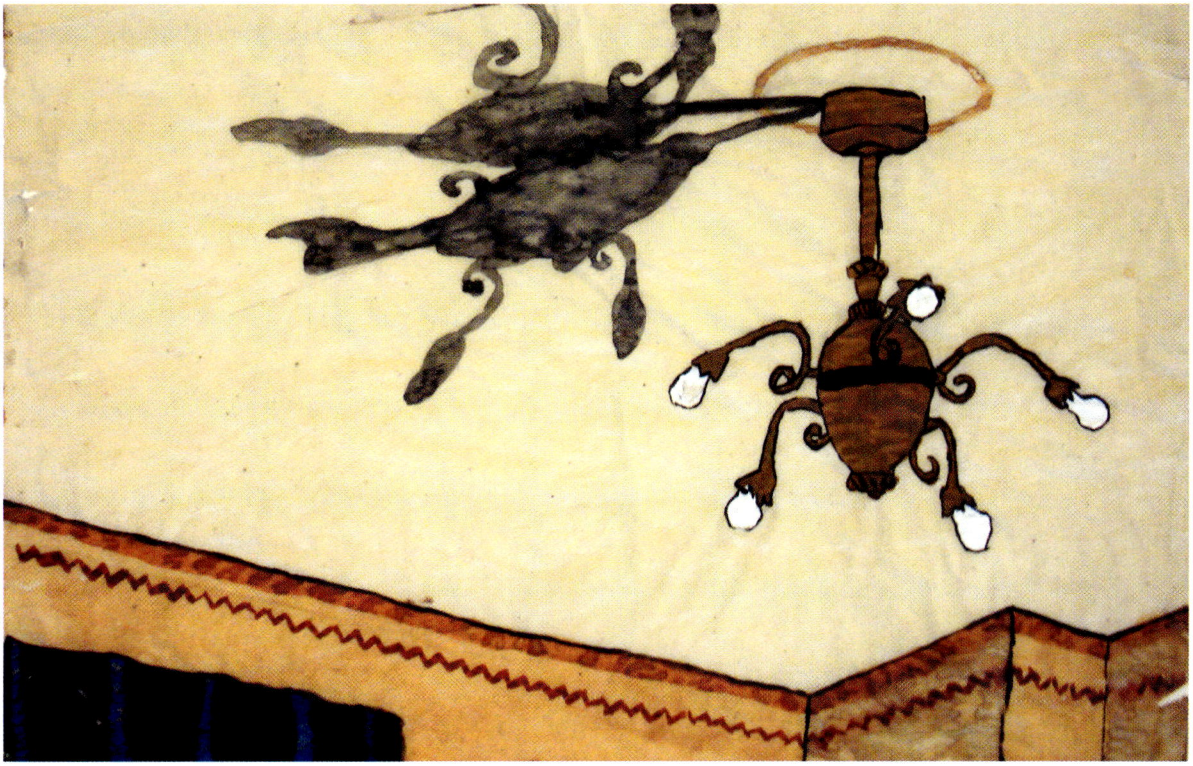

UNFINISHED FIREPLACE

[undated]

watercolor and pencil

12 x 9 inches

Collection Vassar College Library

Bishop's underdrawing has none of the labored aspects of a cartoon. With a soft, sketchy line, she maps out a general sense of the picture. The application of paint redefines it with an authority of its own.

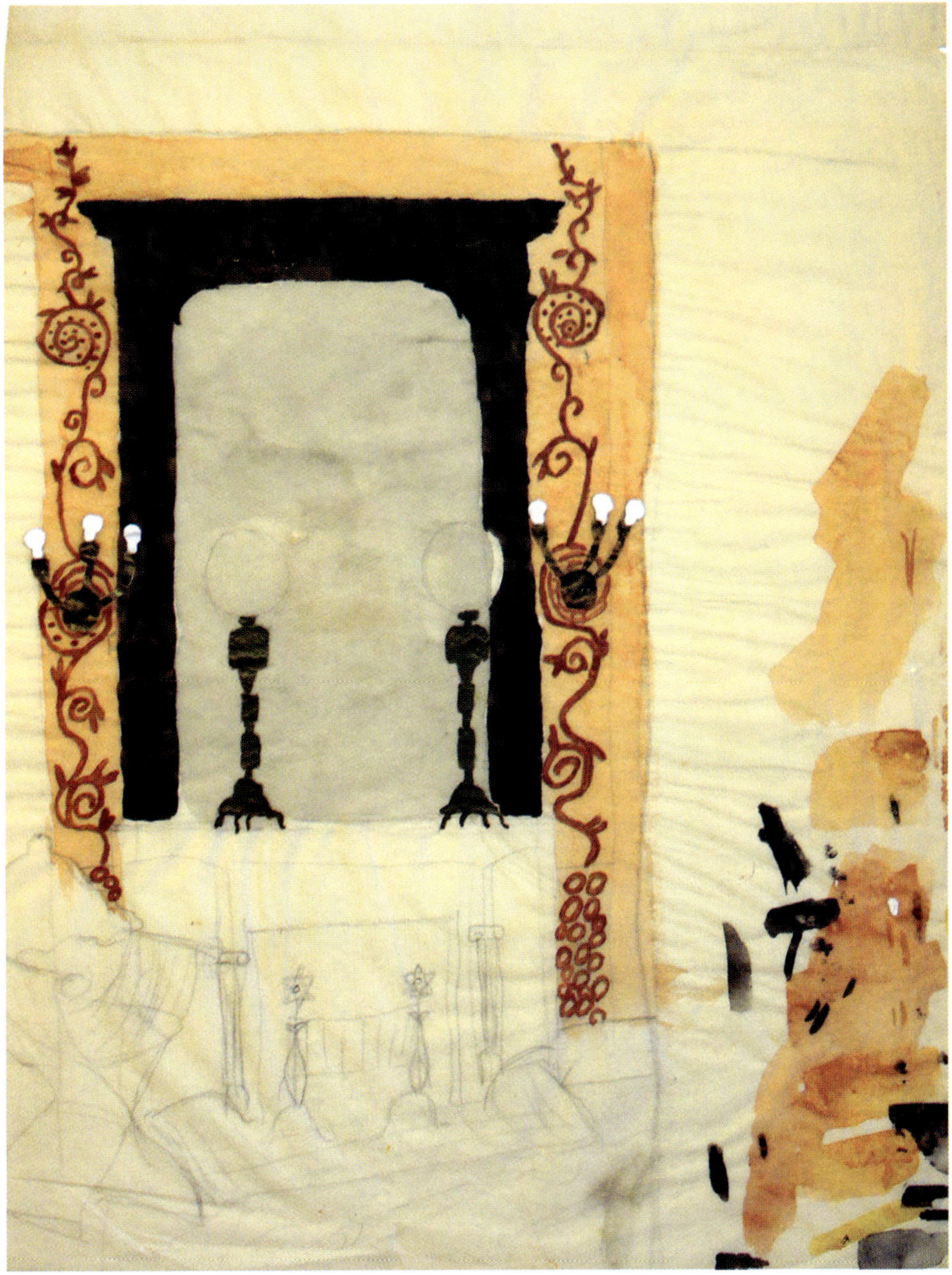

TEA SERVICE

[undated]

crayon

8 x 10 inches

Collection of Alice Methfessel

Tea for one. Signed with the initial "B" on the silver spoon.

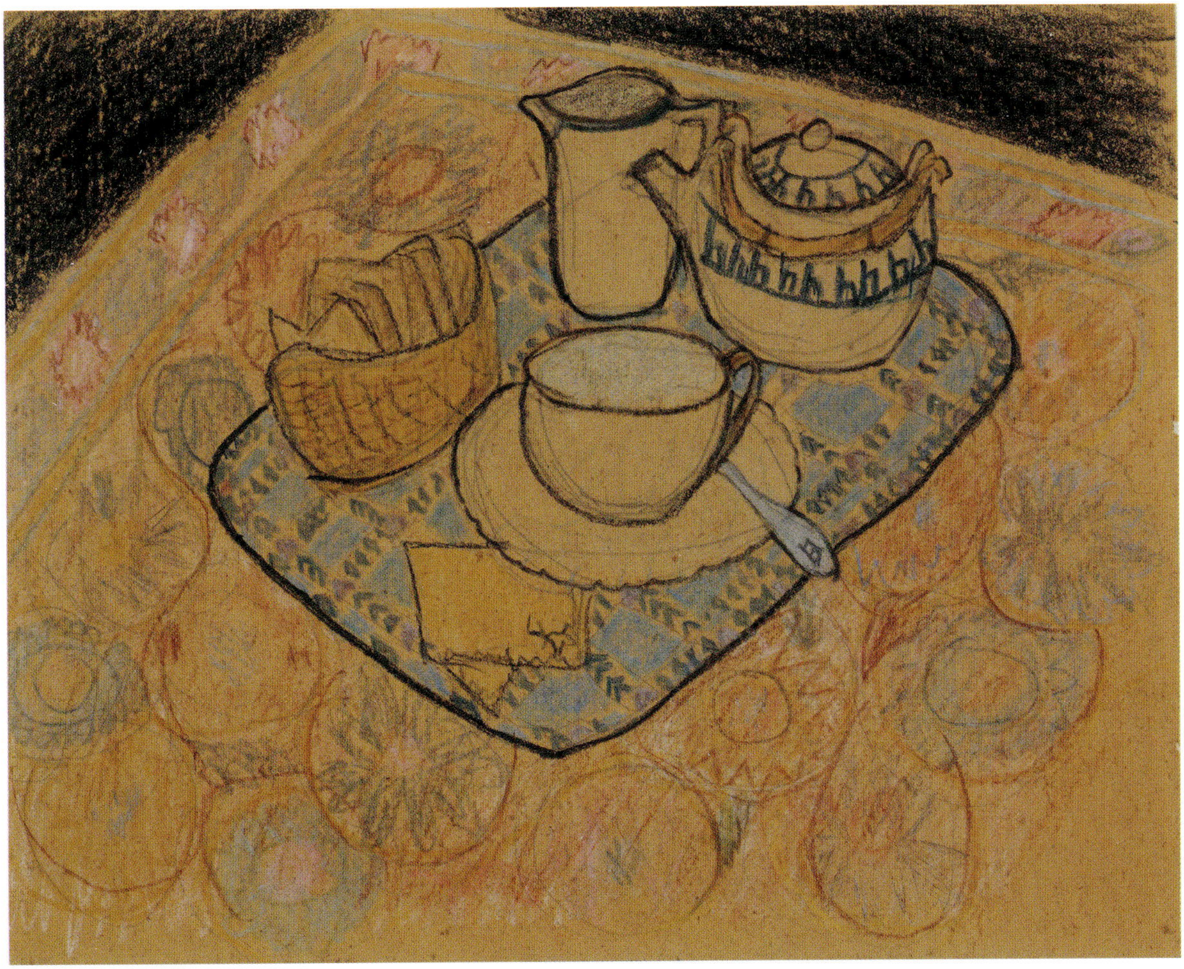

TABLE WITH CANDELABRA

[undated]

watercolor and gouache

7 ½ x 5 ⅞ inches

Collection of Alice Methfessel

The interior view – of tables, flowers, household objects – dominates Bishop's painting. In the domestic iconography a presence develops, the way it does in much of her poetry, where things remain themselves and at the same time suggest deeper associations. In this picture the tablecloth is part landscape, part map, the mirror part self, the newspaper part epic event. Flowers make the room bright; candles imitate a tree.

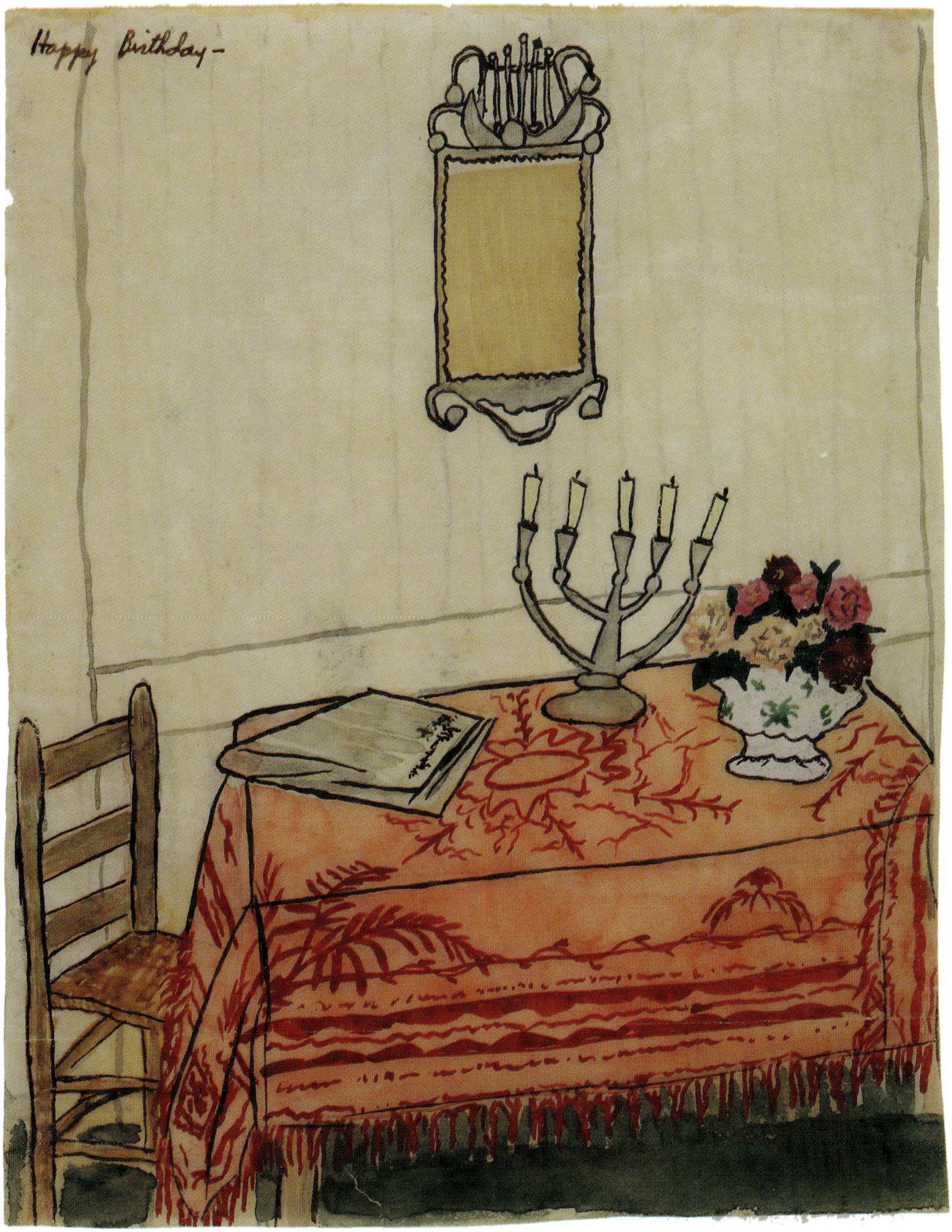
Happy Birthday –

LAMP

[1952]

watercolor, gouache, and ink

10 ¼ x 7 ¼ inches

Collection of Vassar College Library

The inscription reads: *For Lota / Longer than Alladin's burns / Love, & many Happy Returns / March 16th, 1952 / Elizabeth.* From a prominent Brazilian family, Lota (Maria Carlota Costellat de Macedo Soares) was Bishop's lover from 1951 until her suicide in 1967. This painting, with its implication of wishes granted and darkness banished (and its pun on "touching"), dates from their first year together.

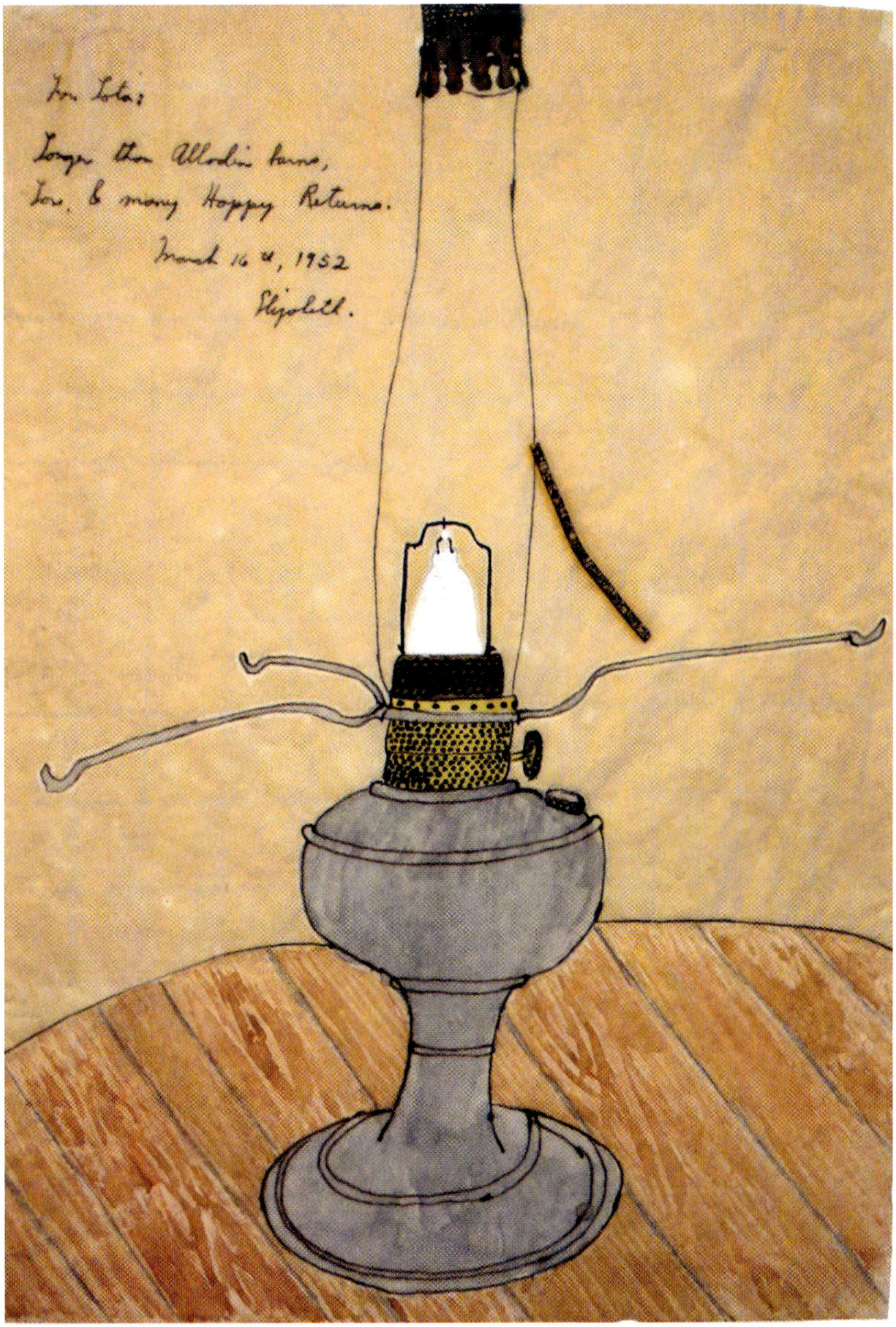
For Lola:
Happy Returns.
March 16th, 1952

BRAZILIAN LANDSCAPE

[*undated*]

watercolor and gouache

whereabouts unknown

This painting belonged to Bishop's doctor Anny Baumann and disappeared after Baumann's death.

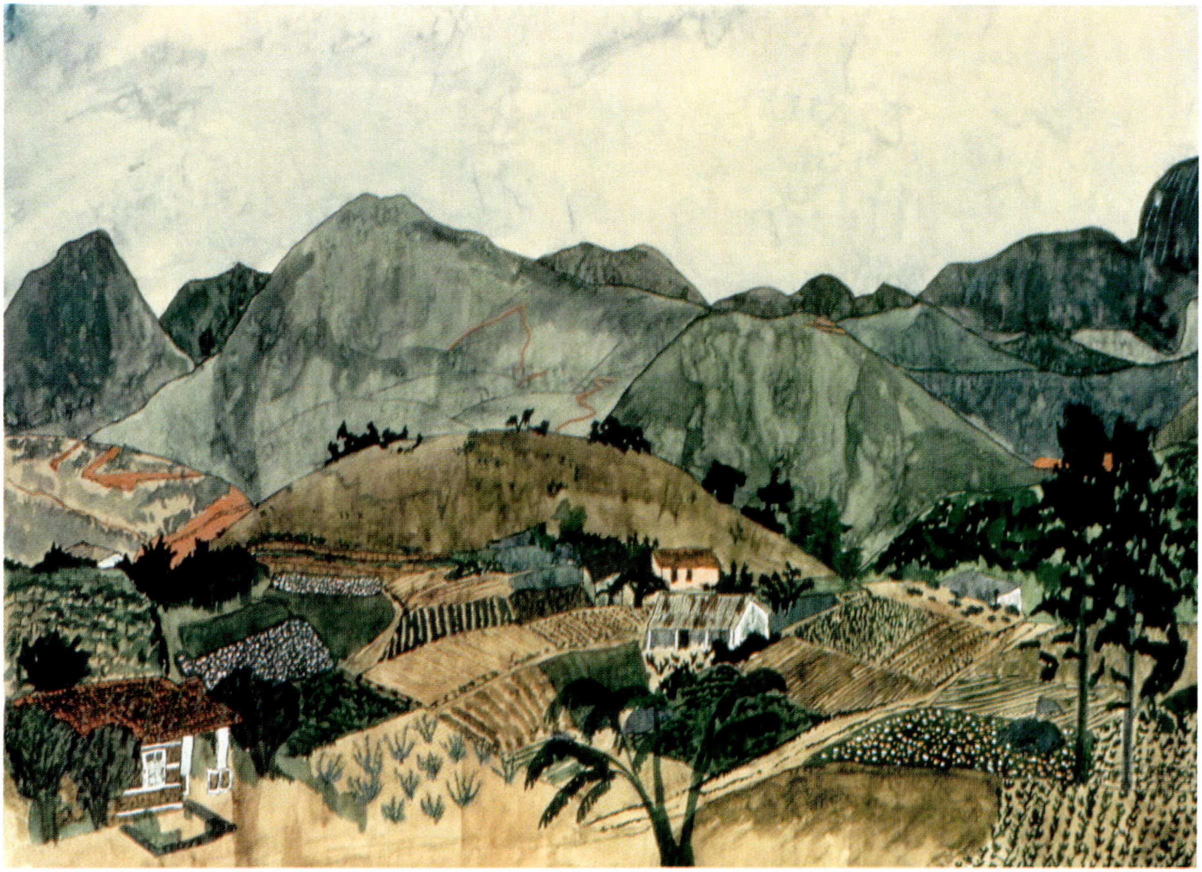

INTERIOR WITH CALDER MOBILE

[undated]

watercolor and gouache

Collection of Vassar College Library

The interior of Samambaia, the house built by Lota (near Petropolis, in the mountains outside Rio de Janeiro), where she and Bishop lived. The painting is inscribed on the bottom right, below the Calder mobile, to Rosinha Leão, a friend of theirs in Brazil.

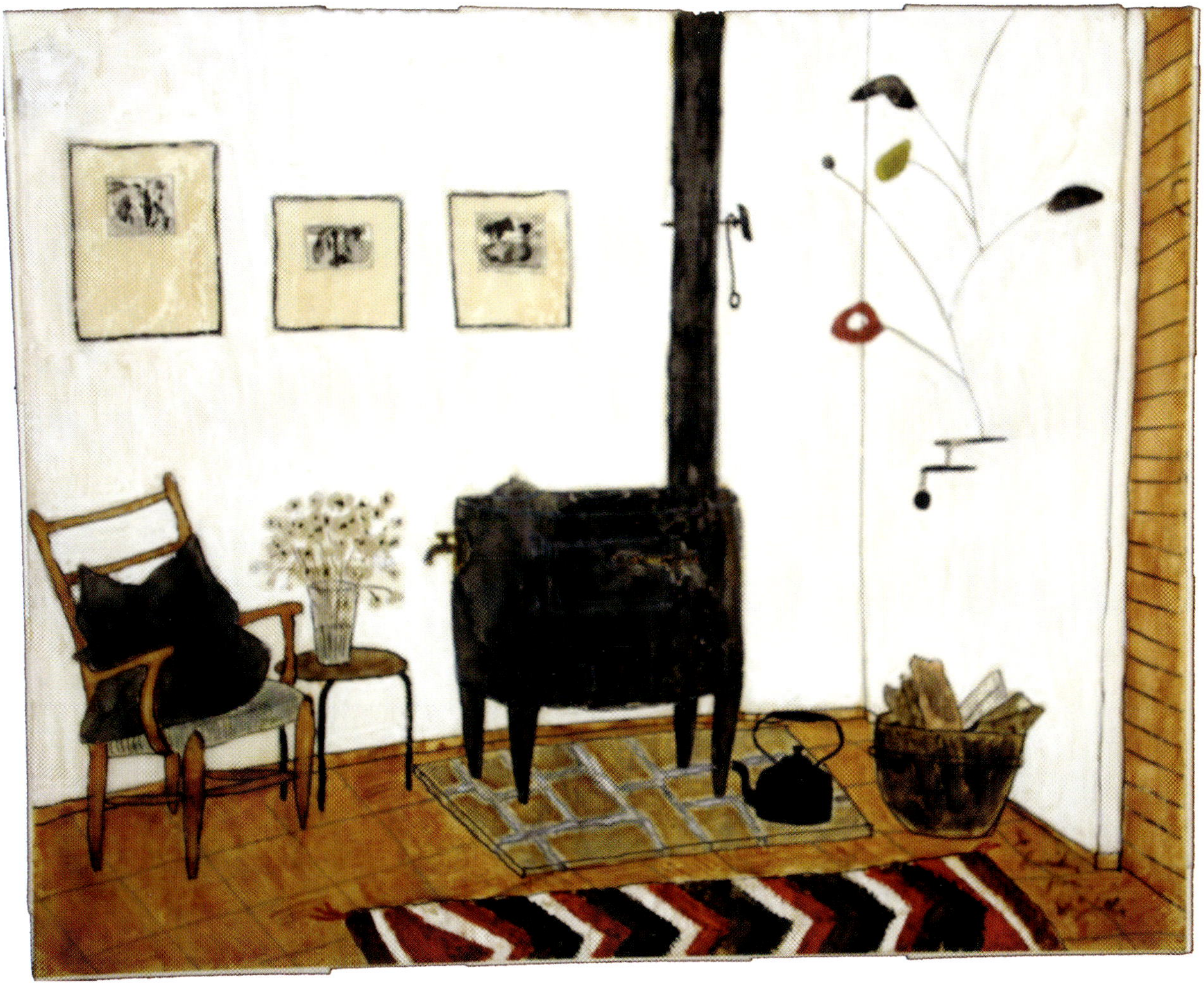

RED STOVE AND FLOWERS

[1955]

watercolor and gouache

Collection of Vassar College Library

The inscription reads: *May the Future's Happy Hours / Bring you Beans & Rice & Flowers / April 27th, 1955 / Elizabeth.* The picture was a birthday present for Magù Leão, a friend in Brazil, whose name appears on the stove. An aggregate of whites plays over a wall of blackness, underlined by one of her specialties: wood grain.

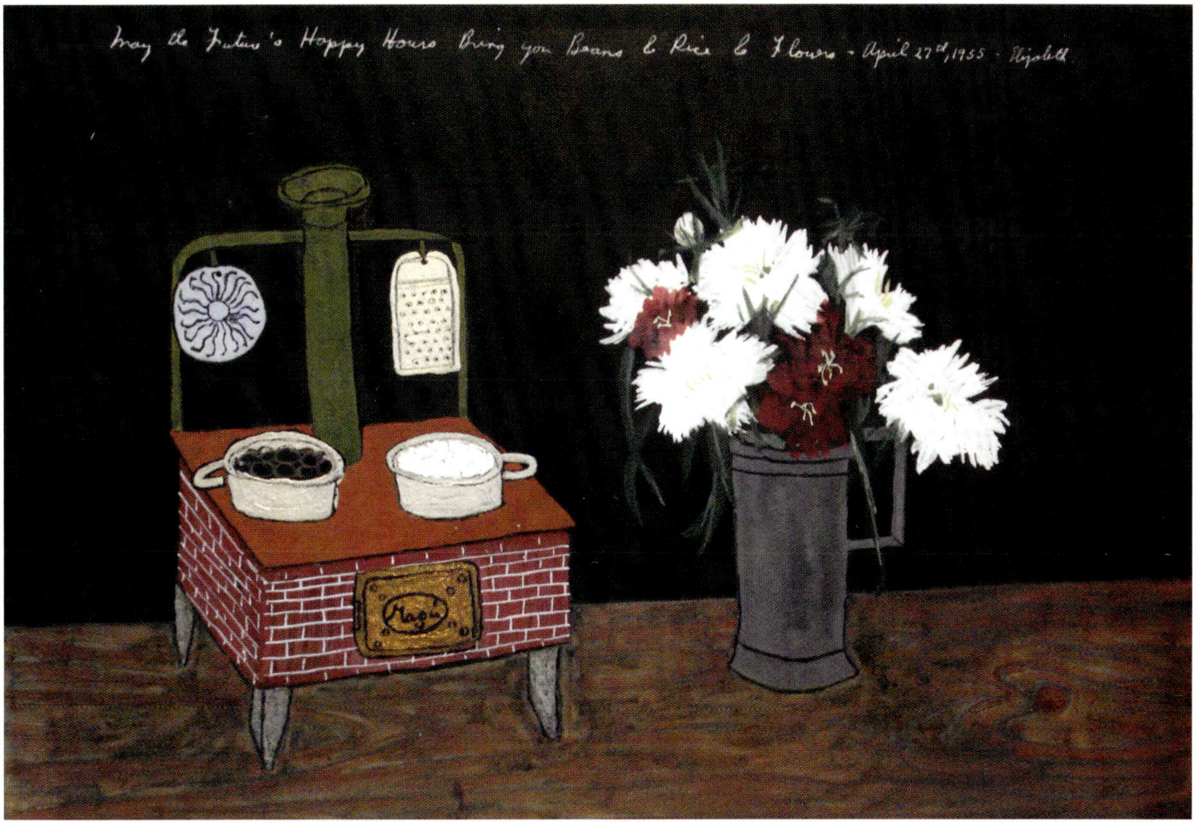
May the Future's Happy Hours Bring you Beans & Rice & Flowers - April 27th, 1955 - Elizabeth

FLOWERS, BOBBY AND ARTHUR

[*undated*]

watercolor and gouache

whereabouts unknown

"Bobby" and "Arthur" are the celebrated duo-pianists and writing team of Robert Fizdale and Arthur Gold. The painting was never given to them.

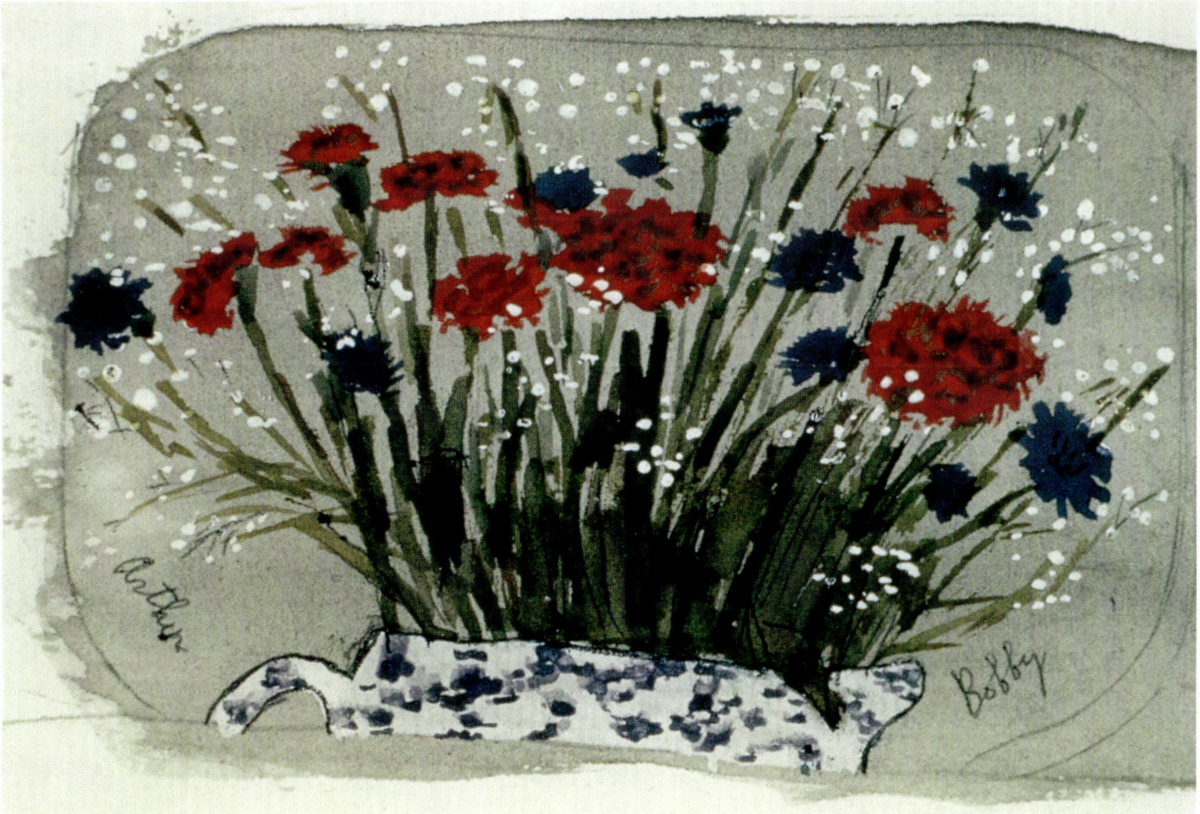
Arthur
Bobby

MEADOW WITH ROCK

[*undated*]

watercolor

whereabouts unknown

This watercolor and the 1963 oil pastel *Coxcombs* are both inscribed to Oscar Simon, a Brazilian friend. Bishop once wrote to Lota: "Oscar just called and said he was coming by to give me a kiss!"

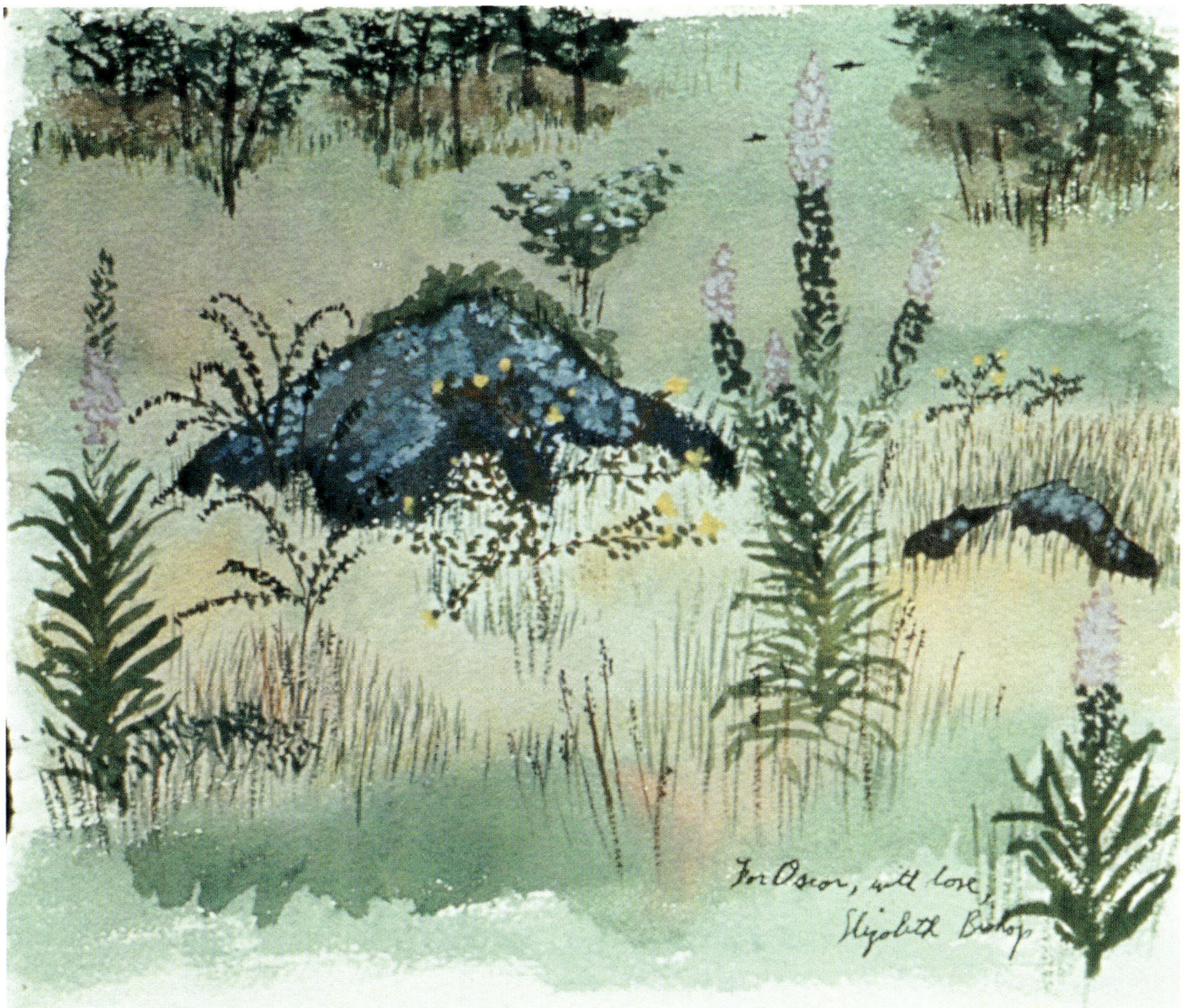
For Oscar, with love,
Elizabeth Bishop

COXCOMBS

[1963]

oil pastel

8 ½ x 10 ½ inches

Collection of Vassar College Library

The flowers, set close to the viewer at the edge of the page, fill the room. The physical energy of Bishop's hand is visible, working colors into one another. Against this exuberance, she has sketched in part of a framed picture on the adjoining wall (a Bissier?), which is gilded with gold paint.

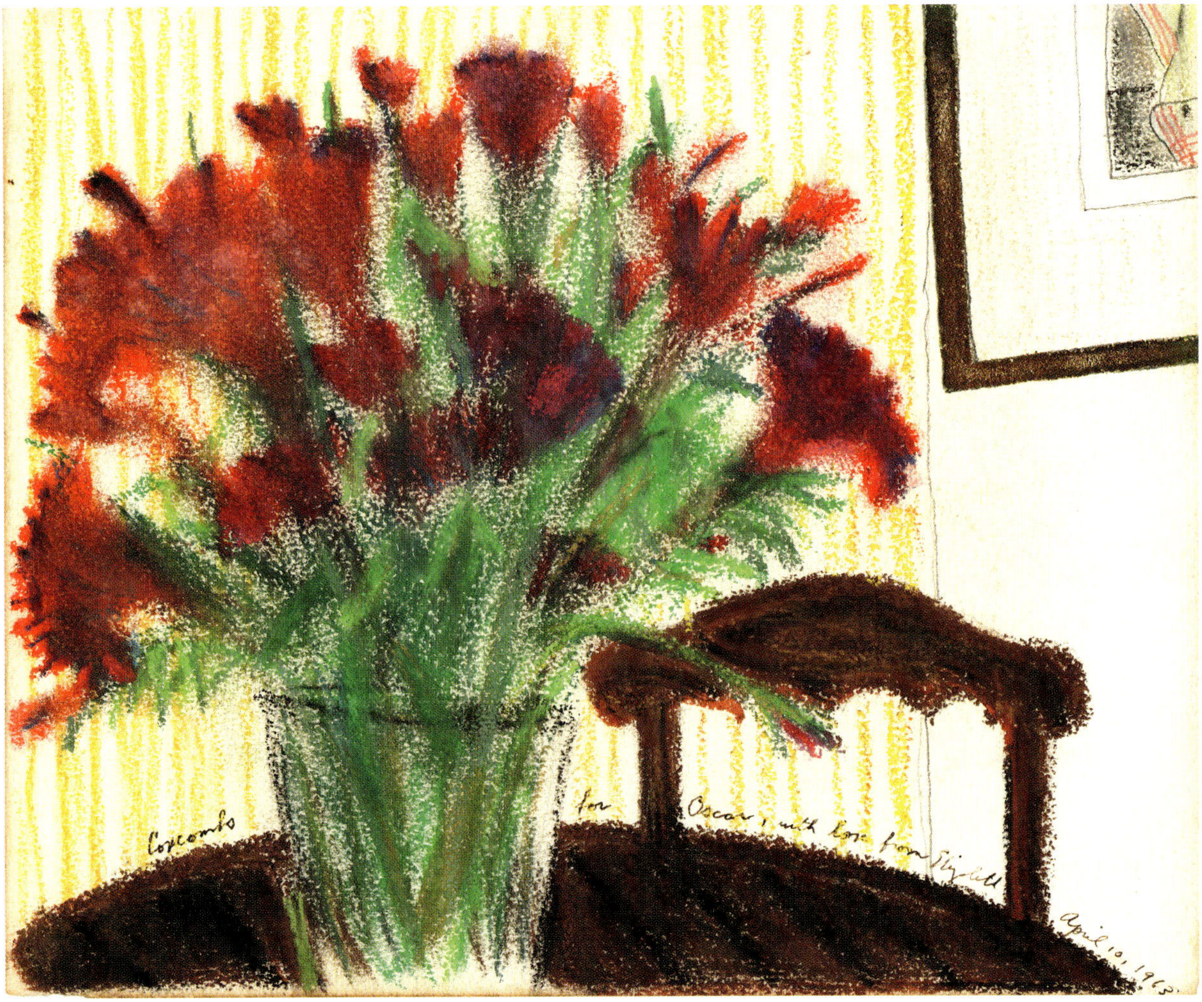
Coxcombs for Oscar, with love from
April 10, 1963.

PANSIES

[1960]

watercolor and gouache

12 ½ x 15 inches

Collection of Alice Methfessel

Ambitious in its realism, it is also, as far as we know, Bishop's largest painting. According to James Jaffe the book beside the basket of flowers is Baedeker's *Northern Italy.* Bishop visited Italy with Louise Crane in 1937 and again with Lota in the late spring of 1964.

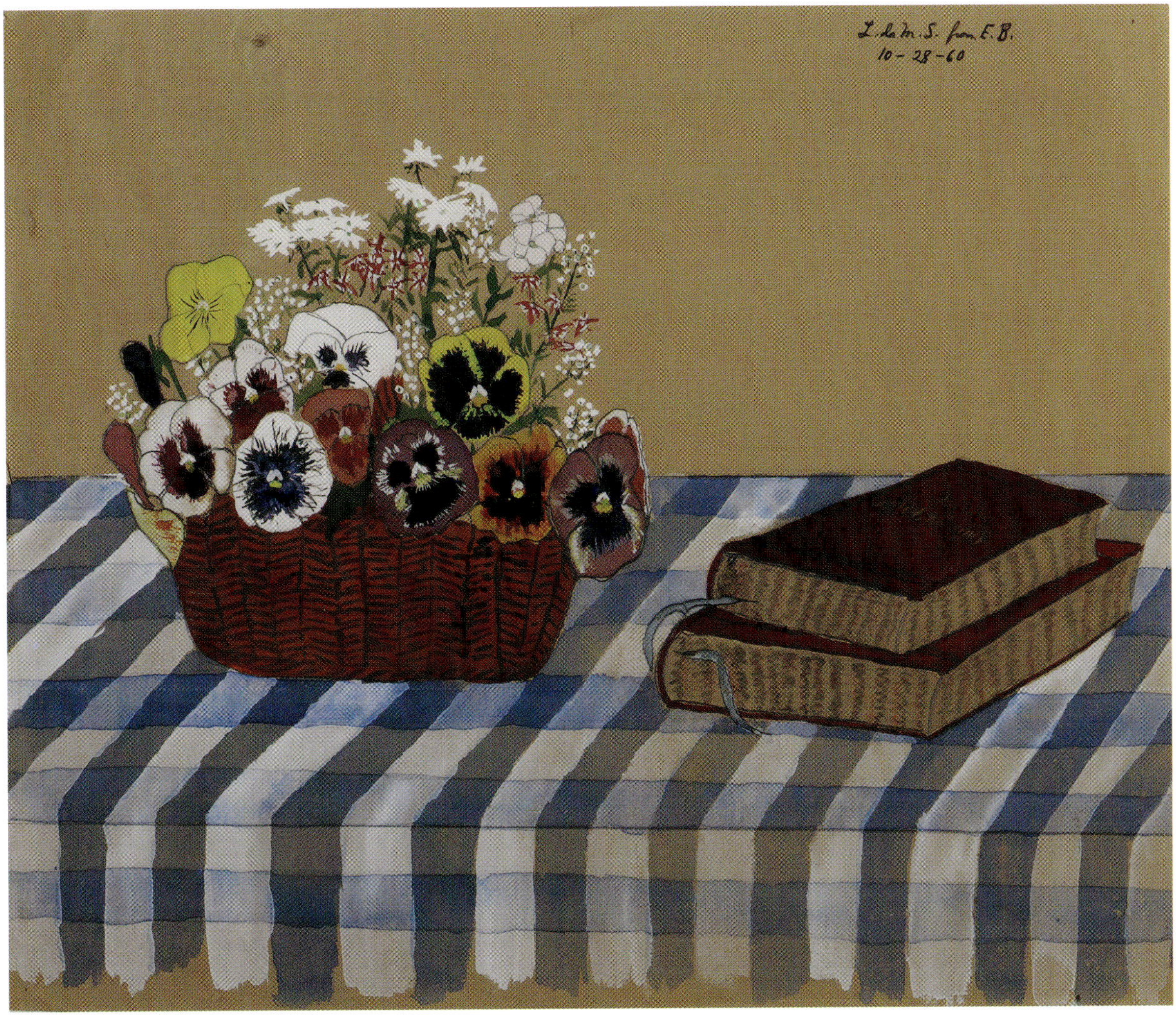
L. de M. S. from E. B.
10-28-60

E. BISHOP'S PATENTED SLOT-MACHINE

[*undated*]

watercolor

10 x 8 inches

Collection of Alice Methfessel

The rainbow arc at the top of the picture – resembling the handle of a suitcase – bears the legend "THE 'DREAM.' " In the diagram of the slot-machine the notations read: "CRYSTAL BALL; SPARK; HANDLE; OPENING IN GLASS CASE." The two sets of numbers are: "2 3 8 10 7 1" and "3 2 5 4 1."

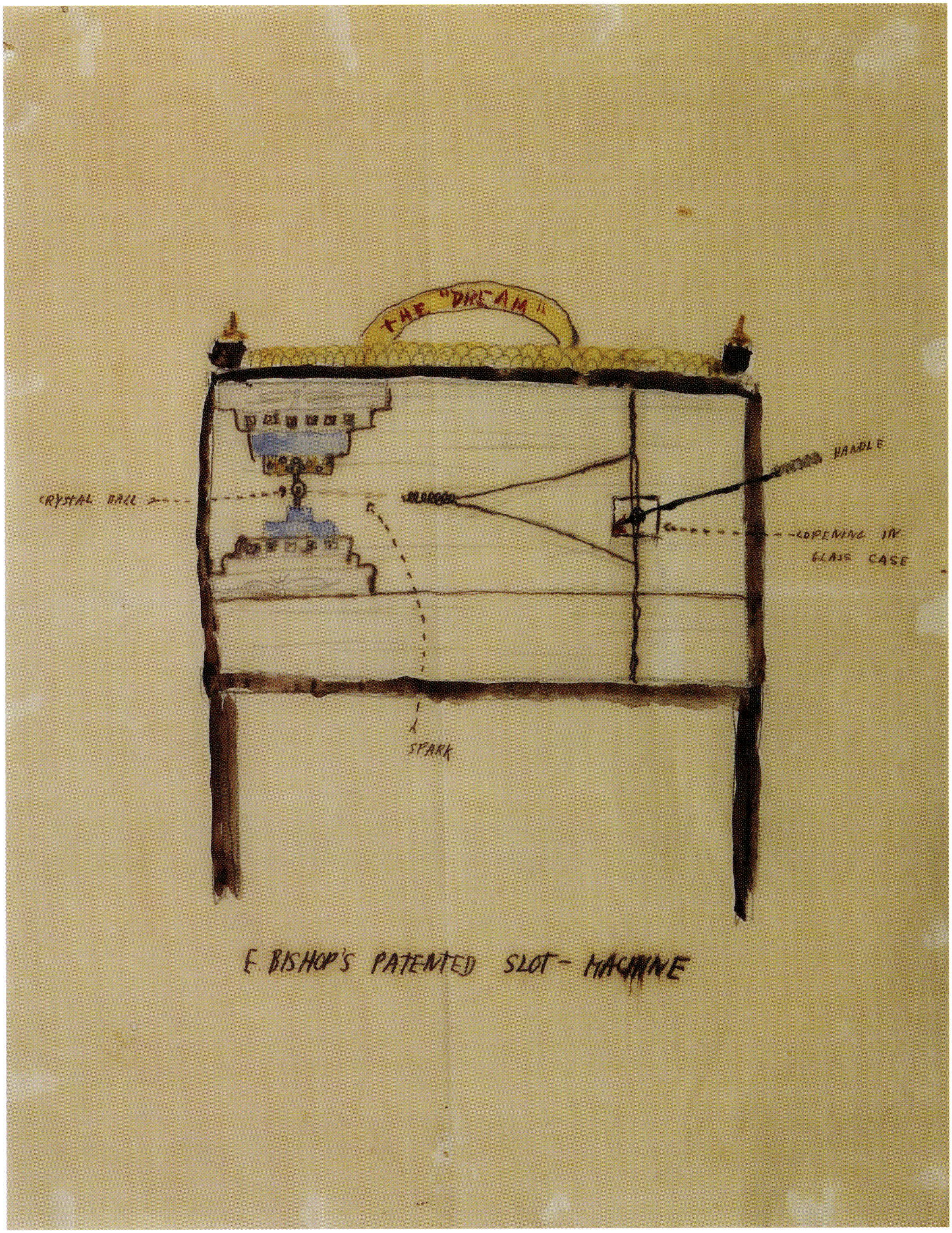
THE "DREAM"
HANDLE
CRYSTAL BALL
OPENING IN
GLASS CASE
SPARK
E. BISHOP'S PATENTED SLOT-MACHINE

RED FLOWERS ON BLACK

[undated]

gouache

9 ¾ x 6 inches

Collection of Alice Methfessel

Devil's paintbrush, painted in Maine a year or two before Bishop's death.

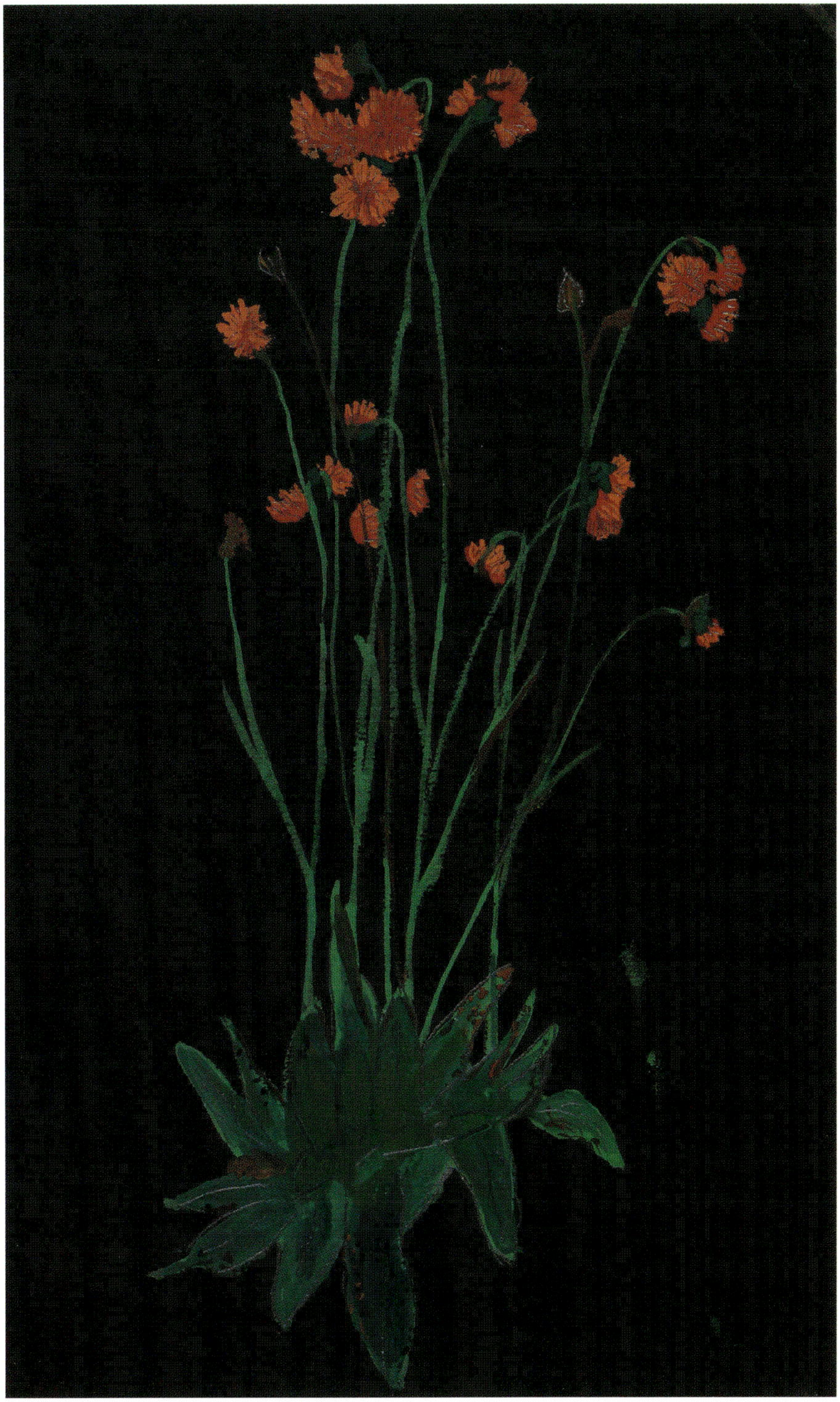

LANDSCAPE WITH GRAY HILLS

[undated]

watercolor, gouache, and ink

4 ¼ x 7 ¼ inches

Private Collection, courtesy Alexandre Gallery, New York; Photo: Takenori Nishijima

Colorists excel in grays. These hills, each differing in shade as well as texture, set the mood of the scene. Under a dull and perhaps cold spring sky, blue smoke rises from the farm house, absorbed into the dark hills. The bleached yellow of the field – a color suffused with brightness – is made brighter by being dotted with white flowers.

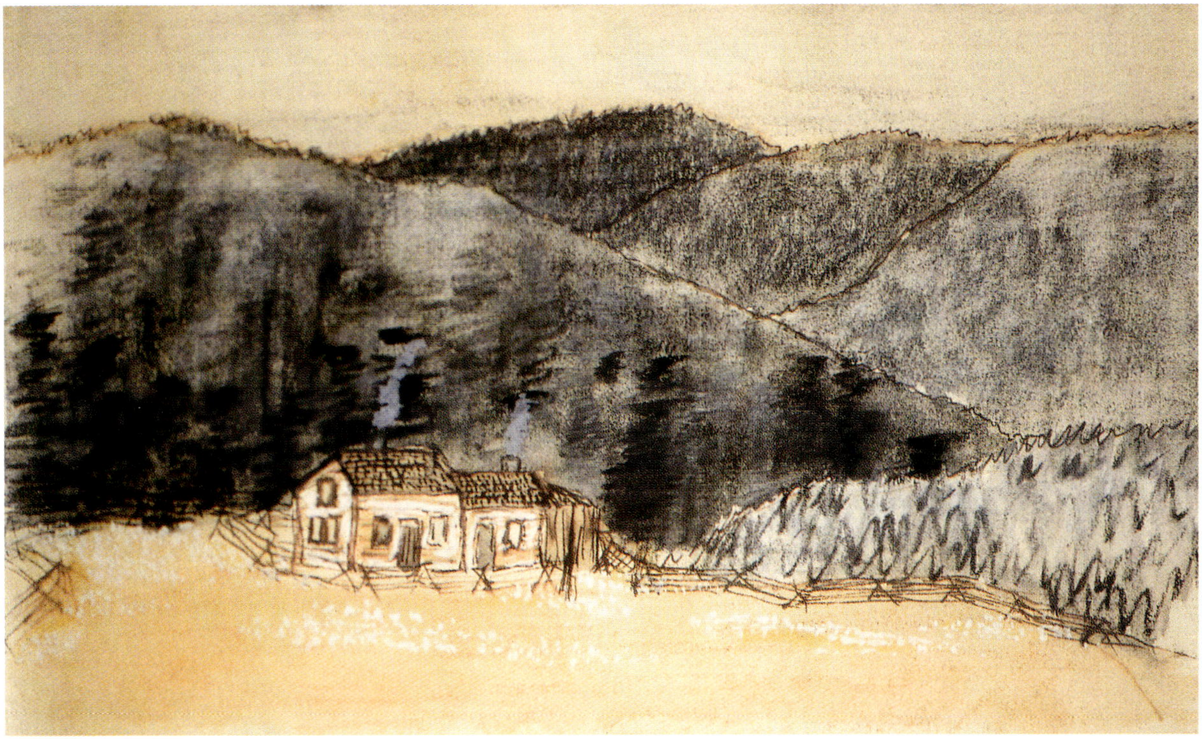

FOUNTAIN

[undated]

pen and ink

3 ½ x 4 ½ inches

Collection of Loren MacIver

CLOCKS AND STOVES

[undated]

pen and ink

2 ¼ x 2 ¼ inches

Private Collection, courtesy Alexandre Gallery, New York

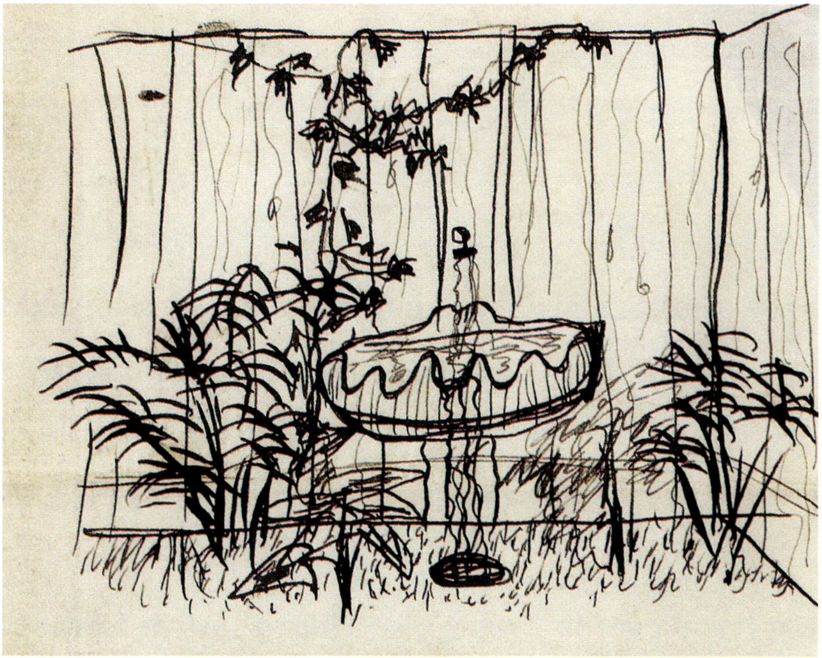

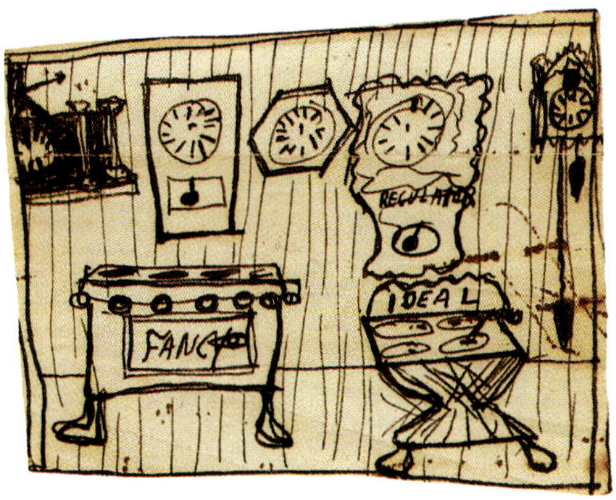
REGULATOR
IDEAL

PROSE

Margaret [Miller] and I are mutually inspiring each other to an exchange of arts, I think. At least I caught her writing a story the other day – a very good one too – and I lean more and more toward watercolors.

By the time school started, I could read almost all of my primer, printed in both handwriting and type, and I loved every word. First, as a frontispiece, it had the flag in full color, with "One Flag, One King, One Crown" under it. I colored in the black-and-white illustrations that looked old-fashioned, even to me, using mostly red and green crayons. On the end pages I had tried to copy the round cancellation marks from old envelopes: "Brooklyn, NY Sept. 1914," "Halifax, Aug. 1916," and so on, but they had not turned out well, a set of lopsided crumbling wheels.

Only the third and fourth grades studied geography. On their side of the room, over the blackboard, were two rolled-up maps, one of Canada and one of the whole world. When they had a geography lesson, Miss Morash pulled down one or both of these maps, like window shades. They were on cloth, very limp, with a shiny surface, and in pale colors – tan, pink, yellow, and green – surrounded by the blue that was the ocean. The light coming in from the windows, falling on the glazed, crackly surface, made it hard for me to see them properly from where I sat. On the world map, all of Canada was pink; on the Canadian, the provinces were different colors. I was so taken with the pull-down maps that I wanted to snap them up, and pull them down again, and touch all the countries and provinces with my own hands. Only dimly did I hear the pupils' recitations of capital cities and islands and bays. But I got the general impression that Canada was the same size as the world, which somehow or other fitted into it, or the other way around, and that in the world and Canada the sun was always shining and everything was dry and glittering. At the same time, I knew perfectly well that this was not true.

We told each other which colors we liked best together, and I remember the feeling of profound originality I experienced when I insisted, although it had just occurred to me, that I had always liked black and brown together best. I saw them floating in little patches of velvet, like the crazy quilts, or smooth little rectangles of enamel, like the paint-sample cards I was always begging for at the general store.

There seemed to be one thing common to all their "primitive" writing, as I suppose it might be called, in contrast to primitive painting; its slipshodiness and haste. Where primitive painters will spend months or years, if necessary, putting in every blade of grass and building up brick walls in low relief, the primitive writer seems in a hurry to get it over with. Another thing was the almost complete lack of detail. The primitive painter loves detail and lingers over it and emphasizes it at the expense of the picture as a whole. But if writers put them in, the details are often impossibly or wildly inappropriate, sometimes revealing a great deal about the writer without furthering the matter in hand at all. Perhaps it all demonstrates the professional writer's frequent complaint that painting is more fun than writing.

Miss Woodhead made a model of "The Landing of the Pilgrims" on a large tabletop. The Rock was the only real thing. Miss Woodhead made the ocean in a spectacular way: she took large sheets of bright blue paper, crumpled them up, and stretched them out over the table. Then, with the blackboard chalk, she made glaring whitecaps of all the points: an ocean grew right before our eyes.

We have been over to see the Hemingways' painting several times. Have you ever seen that wonderful Miró *Farm*? – with everything in it, trees, hens, fences, etc., and a dog barking at footprints.

The first painting I saw by Gregorio Valdes was in the window of a barbershop on Duval Street, the main street of Key West. The shop is in a block of cheap liquor stores, shoeshine parlors and poolrooms, all under a long wooden awning shading the sidewalk. The picture leaned against a cardboard advertisement for Eagle Whiskey, among other window decorations of red-and-green crêpe-paper rosettes and streamers left over from Christmas and the announcement of an operetta at the Cuban school – all covered with dust and fly spots and littered with termites' wings.

It was a view, a real View, of a straight road diminishing to a point through green fields, and a row of straight Royal Palms on either side, so carefully painted that one could count seven trees in each row. In the middle of the road was the tiny figure of a man on a donkey, and far away on the right the white speck of a thatched Cuban cabin that seemed to have the same mysterious properties of perspective as the little dog in Rousseau's *The Cariole of M. Juniot.* The sky was blue at the top, then white, then beautiful blush pink, the pink of a hot, mosquito-filled tropical evening.

That day we bought one of the few pictures he had on hand – a still life of Key West fruits such as a coconut, a mango, sapodillos, a watermelon, and a sugar apple, all stiffly arranged against a blue background. In this picture the paint had cracked slightly, and examining it I discovered an eccentricity of Gregorio's painting. The blue background extended all the way to the tabletop and where the paint had cracked the blue showed through the fruit. Apparently he had felt that since the wall was back of the fruit he should paint it there, before he could go on and paint the fruit in front of it.

Today, my dear, I am entertaining Grant Wood, who wants to see the Valdes picture. He is too depressing, very much like one of his D.A.R. matrons . . . Under the magic spell of all this I have started to paint myself, and yesterday I presented Mrs. Almyda with a picture.

Ancient heroes often have to do penance for and expiate crimes they have committed all unwittingly, and in the same way it seems that some people receive certain "gifts" merely by remaining unwittingly in an undemocratic state of grace. It is a supposition that leaves painting like Gregorio's a partial mystery. But surely anything that is impossible for others to achieve by effort, that is dangerous to imitate, and yet, like natural virtue, must be both admired and imitated, always remains mysterious.

One day she abruptly asked me, "Do you like the *nude,* Elizabeth?" I said yes I did on the whole. Marianne: "Well, so do I, Elizabeth, but in *moderation,*" and she immediately pressed on me a copy of Sir Kenneth Clark's new book, *The Nude,* which had just been sent to her.

The small living room and dining room were crowded with furniture that had obviously come from an older, larger home, and there were many pictures on the walls, a mixture of the old and the new, family possessions and presents from friends (these generally depicted birds or animals). One painting of trees and a stream had suffered an accident to its rather blurry tree passage, and Marianne herself had restored this – I felt, unkindly, not too successfully – with what she said was "Prussian blue."

Well I talked to you, which helped for an hour or so there, but I really don't know what to do any more. If it weren't so bloody hot. Now I'm dreading everything, everything and particularly those few days I have to spend in N.Y. at a hotel alone. The last six months have been a total loss and I don't feel as if I could ever write anything again and I don't want to go on living. I can't work on any of the old things any more and I'm so bloody lonely I think I'll die just of that.

. . . Charles Shooker seemed very proud of having a watercolor hung next to yours at the Brooklyn Museum. He described yours to me very carefully & I was so mad – I'd never even seen it. He's nice – they're all "nice" – it's just me that's wrong, as always. He raves about your picture of Emmett Kelly. Have you finished Cummings? The only painter here I'm really interested in is a very young boy who "works here" – very sweet. He studied with Mark Tobey for five years. He's going to show me his pictures tomorrow.

Well, if I were a painter none of this would ever have happened, or so I keep telling myself.

There is an apple tree here – a very small one that looks exactly like a child's drawing of an apple tree – and not too much unlike mine.

Every night he walked back and forth for a distance of over a mile, in the dark, with his lantern and his stick, and a potato sack on his back to put the papers in – a picturesque sight, in some ways like a Rembrandt.

Let us leave him in his house, at four one morning, his reading selected, the conflagration all over, the lantern shining clearly. It is an extremely picturesque scene, in some ways like a Rembrandt, but in many ways not.

One of the most effective scenes that I have ever seen, for color contrast, was a group of these libertine convicts, in their black and white stripes, spraying, or otherwise tending to, a large clump of tropical shrubbery on the lawn of a public building. There were several varieties of bushes and plants in the arrangement, each of which had either brilliantly colored or conspicuously marked leaves. One bush, I remember, had long knife-like leaves, twisting as they grew into loose spirals, the upper surface of the leaf magenta, the under an ocher yellow. Another had large, flat, glossy leaves, dark green, on which were scrawled magnificent arabesques in lines of chalk-yellow. These designs, contrasting with the bold stripes of the prison uniform, made an extraordinary, if somewhat florid, picture.

The Biennale was thoroughly exhausting, but we had a nice time, even so. As I said, in my note that you may never get, I was quite reconciled to Henry Moore by the two *beautiful* things he had there – *King & Queen* and a reclining woman, in a good old Mayan pose. (I can't say I understand why he brings in Mexico so much in those things for the *Time & Life* building, can you? Except that they're some form of Calendar stones, but that seems both obvious and farfetched.) The English painters I thought were pretty disappointing – one – Scott – makes one feel, "My god! what rationing has done!" I think I almost like Partick Heron and his snarls of twine best of them all. There were many too many paintings from most countries. A couple of ravishing Marinis. Fortunately we got there rather late and almost everything good had been sold to rich São Paulo coffee planters – otherwise I don't think Lota – who adores to buy things – would ever be able to leave Brazil for the rest of her life. She could only get two Kokoschka lithographs; and I bought a drawing by a young American I know and like. But she is determined to get a classic figure, about six feet high, twisted bronze, draped in a toga, by Mascherini – know him? – to put on the corner of the terrace here. Even if I find the *feet* a little *chichi* I don't blame her a bit. It is lovely, really – a young Paulista had reserved it, but he may well change his mind. I'm afraid if he does that you will not see me or Lota for a couple more years.

I think Herbert Read is an esthetic glutton – he just has to understand and feel the "significance" of everything, regardless, and mentally he is an enormous fat man eating away indiscriminately.

. . . it has been one of my dreams that someday someone would think of Vermeer, without my saying it first, so now I think I can die in a fairly peaceful frame of mind, any old time, having struck the best critic of poetry going that way.

Another place I like very much and wish I just owned is the Dumbarton Oaks museum – just the right size. And if you're ever in the National Gallery take a look at the Delacroix of a little Algerian girl for me – it's one of their best paintings, I think. I tried and tried to write a poem about it but never succeeded. Also a beautiful Gauguin landscape of Brittany, spring-like – oh there are lots of things, of course.

Uncle Neddy stands on an imaginary dark red carpet, against a dun-colored wall. His right arm rests on the back of a small chair. This chair is a holy wonder; it must have been the painter's "property" chair – at least, I never saw anything like it in my grandmother's house. It consists of two hard-looking maroon-colored pads, both hung with thick, foot-long, maroon fringes; the lower one makes the seat, the upper one, floating in the airless air, and on which Uncle Neddy's arm rests, the back. Uncle Neddy wears a black suit, velveteen, I think; the jacket has pockets and is gathered to a yoke. He has a narrow white collar and white cuffs and a double black bow of what appears to be a grosgrain ribbon is tied under the jacket collar. Perhaps his face is more oblivious than calm. Its not actually belonging to the suit or the chair gives it an extraneous look. It could almost have drifted in from another place, or another year, and settled into the painting. Plump (he was never in the slightest plump, that I can remember), his hair parted neatly on the left, his cheeks as pink as a girl's, or a doll's. He looks rather more like his sisters than Uncle Neddy – the later versions of him, certainly. His tight trousers come to just below the knee and I can make out three ornamental buttons on each side. His weight rests on the left leg; his right leg is crossed in front of it and the toe of his right boot barely touches the other boot and the red carpet. The boots are very small, buttoned. In spite of his peaceful expression, they probably hurt him. I remember his telling me about the copper-toed boots he wore as a child, but these have no copper toes and must be his "good" boots. His body looks neatly stuffed. His eyes are a bright hazel and in the left one – right, to me – the painter has carefully placed a highlight of dry white paint, like a crumb. He never looked so clean and glossy, so peaceful and godly, so presentable, again – or certainly not as I remember him.

Loren [MacIver] is also sorry to have missed meeting you. I don't believe you took the catalogue along, so I'm sending one. I called up the gallery yesterday just to find out for myself how much things cost. There's one small fairly old one that I want very much if I can possibly afford it, to take back with me. While I was at it I asked the prices of the recent ones I'd liked particularly, so I've jotted them down here just to give you an idea. The *Rue Mouffetard* painting is a beauty – long and narrow, in a slightly earlier style – thick paint and wonderful bright little details, fragments of letters, etc. (I don't like the collage of the same street so much.) Also the *Hellenic Landscape* I liked very much – all gray-blues, and those tiny buildings also have letterings on them, fragments of advertisements, in Greek of course. It has much more depth and feeling than that bad reproduction gives any idea of. The big one, not shown, called *Acropolis* – pillars that cross the canvas completely, at one side, and mysterious fragments at the other – I've been told by those who know much better than I do, is one of her finest. I think I still prefer the smaller one, but I'm no kind of judge, and have no idea what you'd like, or what you have in mind, or whether they strike you as too expensive, etc. etc. (I'm not telling you about the little one I want for myself!)

We went to São Paulo for the opening of the Biennale this year. They invited us and paid our hotel bills, so we really could relax and have a lovely time! Thousands of abstractions – horribly depressing after a few hours – but a few very good things – folk stuff from Bahia, a wonderful show, the Burle-Marx was good, and Francis Bacon and Mies van der Rohe.

But (perhaps I've said this before) if after I read a poem, the world looks like that poem for 24 hours or so, I'm sure it's a good one – and the same goes for paintings. I studied a huge book on Bosch I have for several days – and the world looked like Bosches for a month afterwards – not that it really doesn't anyway, these days. Then recently here I saw a Jules Bissier show (do you know his paintings? – slight, maybe, but beautiful) and the world looked all like Bissiers for a long time, here, there, and everywhere.

While we were away, the cook took up painting – proving that art only flourishes in leisure time, I guess – and has turned out to be a really wonderful primitive, so we shall probably soon start peddling her on 57th St. & making our fortunes. We found a large rock painting she had done – a bird – using a big lichen as part of his body. We are afraid to comment too much for fear she'll begin on the walls. Lota told her to please *clean* the garbage pail – she is half-savage and very dirty, although a fine cook – and ten minutes later we found it painted in violent reds and pinks and blacks.

At last I am mailing you a picture. However, I am not very well pleased with it. I'm afraid, to use an elegant expression, I bit off more than I could chew. However, it's big enough so that if you like any section of it you can cut that part out; and I'm doing some more smaller ones and if any turn out well I'll send you another one. The one I'm sending is from Lota's road, looking down over the land belonging to a florist, just below us – a very nice neighbor to have . . .

On second thought I realize now I should have sent you one of the cook's paintings instead of mine. Hers are getting better and better, and the rivalry between us is intense – if I paint a picture she paints a bigger and better one; if I cook something she immediately cooks the same thing, only using up *all* the eggs.

The cook was wonderful but it finally got to be a choice between Art and Peace, and tranquility seemed more important than a masterpiece every afternoon.

We are having a real, old-fashioned stove made for one end – but "modern"-looking at the same time. Near it goes a Calder now in Rio – the only busy touch – the clavichord is on one wall, and a small early picture of Loren's I brought with me; I also bought Lota a Schwitters for her birthday. So you see your small picture will fit right in that intimate atmosphere, only I wish it were you instead.

The day before we had had the Calders here and that visit was more successful, I'm afraid. They've spent some time in Brazil before, and they *love* to *samba*.

Calder went sambaing all over the terrace, wearing a bright orange shirt, just like a calendula swaying in the breeze.

Calder has left us the biggest pair of blue jeans I have ever seen and a red flannel shirt. We do like them (the Calders) so much. He composed a small poem one day after I had tactlessly suggested a *nap* – or maybe it was what I said:

If you've had too much booze,
You can take a little snooze.

. . . Carnival's one big glorious mess, but a more orderly and artistic mess, really. I was in Amazonas this year, but Lota went with the Calders, and it *rained*. The beautiful Louis XV costumes were all draggled, but they danced on until dawn. Calder stood up and watched for six hours – he is made of iron like one of his own creations, I think.

I brought back a tuba from Ouro Prêto – a huge one. It looks big enough for any two Brazilian band players to march inside. It is from the old town band and it was a shame it was being sold, but since it was, I bought it. Alberto polished for two days straight – it was almost black. Now, gleaming and beautiful, it is hung on the wall and looks very nice against old bricks.

I did – do – like early Chirico – but "The Weed" was influenced, if by anything, by a set of prints I had of Max Ernst – lost long ago – called *Histoire Naturelle* (something like that) in which all the plants, etc., had been made by frottage – on wood, so the wood grain showed through.

Well, off to show my "secretary" the Frick and the Guggenheim.

I went to the Gardner Museum – hadn't been there for 20 years or so – what a crazy home it must have been – but the Vermeer and the flowers were wonderful.

You fly from Lima straight to Rio – I've done it by day and by night – the Andes are frightening, but the day flight is worth it, I think. You'll see how exactly like some of Klee's paintings they look . . .

. . . it was a lovely & fascinating & surprising weekend & all your art works haunt my dreams.

Frani took me to the Storm King Art Center. Thirteen David Smiths dotted around the grounds, among other things – a very funny and nice *The Lady Artist* of David Smith – do you know it?

There is a magnificent view of Penobscot Bay and islands, and those schooners that now take people on cruises sail by from time to time – very Marinish. (He painted around here, so that's to be expected, I suppose.)

Yesterday I actually got out my watercolors and designed my own book jacket for the book of poems that will come out, I hope, next fall. It's to be called *Geography III,* and looks like an old-fashioned schoolbook, I hope.

I was trying to remember your E.B. cozy-corner and I'm not sure whether you have – or if you don't, if you'd care for – one of my genuine primitive paintings. I'll be glad to send you my next work of art – and surely, now I'm not teaching for a while, I'll have time to paint some pictures – even think of a poem, possibly.

I had to go to Rockland on the ferry last week and listened in on a long conversation – narcissistic monologue, rather – by a rather handsome young painter (bad painter, from what I saw when I peeked into his van). He's been coming here since childhood, but . . . talked away about Puget Sound, Seattle, and where he teaches art (I don't know where). He also *runs.* I was very tempted to enter into his monologue but just eavesdropped for an hour while he went on & on about the difference in ART on the East Coast & the West Coast.

I have the most beautiful bouquet of "spring flowers" I have ever seen – honestly. If I had my paints with me I'd even attempt to do you a small watercolor or gouache of them – and I still may if I can get them home safely tomorrow. Daffodils, small iris, daisies (two kinds and sizes), yellow snapdragon, pink snapdragon, and eight rose-red tulips, just now opening . . .

My god (as you'd say!) it's AWFUL to be so old – it seems all of a sudden, although of course it couldn't be! Thank you for the beautiful lovely flowers – they at least are young!

AFTERWORD

The critical response that followed the publication of *Exchanging Hats* was almost unanimous in its praise of Bishop's accomplishment as an artist. The book was chosen by John Russell, in the *New York Times Book Review,* as number two on his top-ten list of art books for 1996. Holland Cotter, in the daily *New York Times,* saw in her pictures "traces of a sharply observant eye ever on the move, limned in an aptly evanescent medium." In the London *Independent,* Lavinia Greenlaw wrote, "Her use of colour is as subtly dramatic as her style of composition. . . The skies in her pictures radiate or oppress, never blue but ranging from apricot to old envelope. She is as particular and demanding of colour as she is of all sensory effects." Jamie McKendrick, in the London *Times Literary Supplement* referred to her paintings of landscapes and buildings as "powerfully atmospheric and original works."

Curiously, one of the few negative notes was sounded by a poet and literary critic. In an appraisal of Bishop's paintings that weaves together insights into her poetry, William Logan, writing in *The New Criterion,* stated, "Her watercolors . . . never got any better in three decades of practice, and there's no sign she thought to take lessons."

Logan's condescension may be partly obligatory in comparing Bishop's pictures to her acclaimed poems. Yet, criticism like this – often predicated on the single misapprehension that an artist's *rendering* skills determine her legitimacy – has less to do with art than with a schism of discernment that runs through contemporary culture. "My kid could do that," they say. Encountered in the shimmering world of poets, it has a reactionary feel, as if in Bishop's fresh and anything-but-academic pictures an unstated boundary had been overstepped, unleashing a show of retrenchment in the close ranks of a conservative order.

In 1969, John Ashbery wrote, "Miss Bishop is somehow an establishment poet . . . and the establishment ought to give thanks; she is proof that it can't be all bad." In the late sixties, achievements of formalism in poetry, however prismatic, were met by a sullen disdain from a vanguard of poets who "gathered from the air a live tradition," and for whom the Abstract Expressionist painters were important exemplars. These days a diffuse and less emphatically divided community of poets has been tilted in the other direction, in part by a geometric proliferation of writing workshops, while Mr. Ashbery has become an establishment unto himself. In these seesawing ironies, it's as if Bishop, with her little pictures, has found a way to persist in not being misunderstood.

Throughout her life Bishop collected art and wrote about it in poems, letters, and stories. Many of her friends were artists. She owned a Calder mobile and bought for Lota, her Brazilian partner, a collage by Kurt Schwitters. She made "boxes" in homage to the sculptor Joseph Cornell, and the title of her painting *E. Bishop's Patented Slot-Machine* is a reference to his work.

It's worth observing that none of the art of these three major figures – Calder, Schwitters, and Cornell – depends in any overt way on conventional draftsmanship or painting ability. As Georges Bataille writes somewhere, "Realism gives me the impression of a mistake." Rendering skills are not difficult to come by; most students begin *un*learning them their first year of art school. But importantly, modernism itself was for Bishop and others of her generation the heroic model of that unlearning. A profound impatience with an outdated diction produced Matisse and Picasso – as well as William Carlos Williams.

The style of Bishop's painting is a style she settled on. One proof of this is that we have no transitional examples, no works that exhibit the obvious tendencies of a beginner, like trying out ways to turn the form. The coherence of her pictures supersedes a constraint to "get the nose right." In early paintings dating from the thirties and forties such as *Sha Sha, Sleeping Figure,* and *Interior with Extension Cord,* she clearly understands that value lies less in precise replication than in a personal system of marking. As she observes in "Poem," from *Geography III*:

In the foreground
a water meadow with some tiny cows,
two brushstokes each, but confidently cows.

Only about forty of Bishop's pictures, mostly watercolor and gouache, have survived. Her influences were diverse. She liked Édouard Vuillard, Jules Bissiers, Oskar Kokoshka. Paul Klee, who worked small in an ersatz primitive style, was a major influence. She once wrote to James Merrill about flying over the Andes: "You'll see how exactly like some of Klee's paintings they look . . ." Her picture *Brazilian Landscape,* a view from the back porch of Samambaia, the house in Petropolis where she and Lota lived from 1951 to 1967, was sent to a friend with the comment, ". . . it's big enough so that if you like any section of it you can cut that part out." This is an example of her famous modesty – but also perhaps a subtle allusion to her use of Klee's compositional grids, built up out of discrete sections.

Bishop is fluent within her powers. Nothing is tentative – the line may wobble, but it rules. In pictures like *Harris School, The Armory,* and *Daisies in Paint Bucket,* the composition is bold and frontal, with deft touches like the small black-and-white abstraction of a sign on a building, or gray washes that evoke the shiny surface of a paint bucket.

By the time modernism reached its saturation point in mid-century, with Pollock leading the great graduating class of New York's Cedar Tavern into imminent glory, Bishop was living in Brazil. The fact that she was somewhere other than New York for what was, by many estimates, the defining era in the history of American art, rhymes quietly with the habits and predilections of her life. The huge canvases and vivid, autobiographical swagger of abstract expressionism would have been at odds with her own impulses.

Bishop's paintings have much more in common with the work of a later generation of artists, who found in the post-modernism of the sixties and seventies the possibility of new ways of returning to figurative art. Bishop's remarkable *Porthole,* from the 1950s, is similar enough to *Celeste #3,* painted some twenty years later by the young Bay Area artist Joan Brown that the two works could be sequential frames in a graphic novel. Tired of sitting around the apartment, a young woman packs her bags and catches the first boat to Rio.

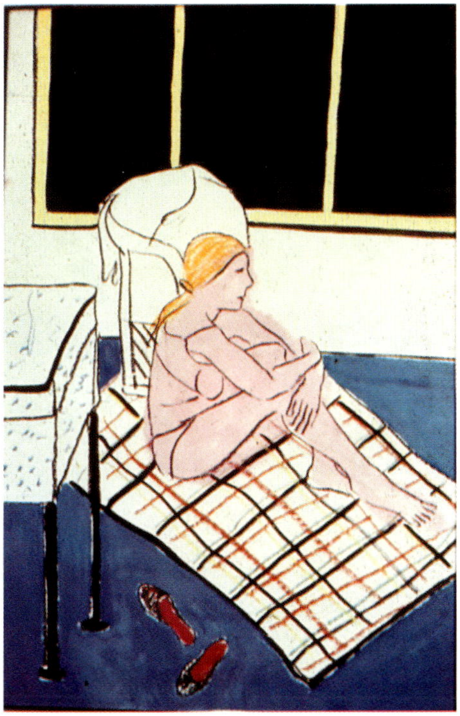

Joan Brown, *Celeste # 3,* 1976

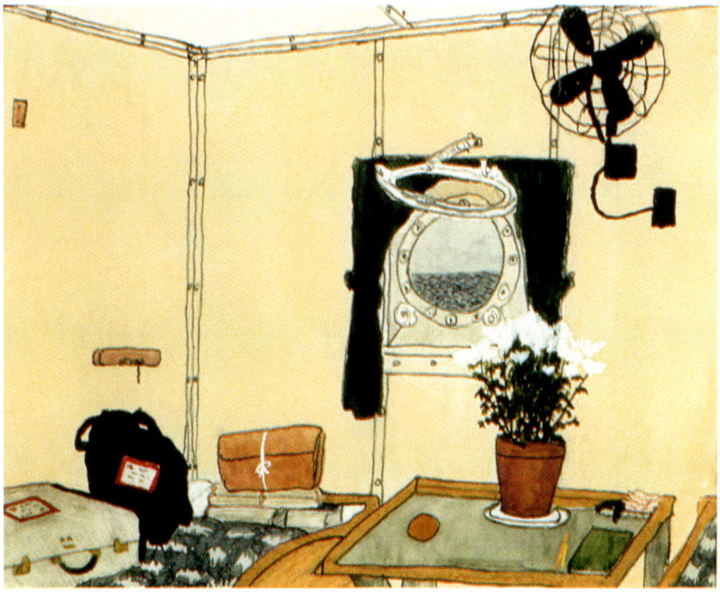

Elizabeth Bishop, *Porthole,* undated

Bishop enjoyed being innovative and invisible at the same time. As a painter, she discovered in the limited range of her skills an intrinsic value. To see it made it so. She was the *elect* of a primitive style – not a supplicant. Aware of permission and rightness, she understood the *form*.

From "The Man-Moth" to "The Moose," the deceptive conventionality of Bishop's poetry is part of what makes it so original, and even subversive. She was the fascinating outsider at the masked ball in a company of congenial, if often over-bred, bores. She opened and admired their jeweled music boxes and, with the real daring of upward mobility, let herself be mistaken for one of them – by *herself* even. Hence that half-modest, half-elitist lilt when she protests that her paintings are, ". . . Not Art – NOT AT ALL."

Her pictures, the way we know of them almost as much as what they are, place us to some extent in a position of reckoning their virtues beyond the guideposts of objective categories. Yet at a certain point in looking at art, categories become useless. Bishop's paintings put a value on the unrehearsed oneness of experience. The elusive strength of her poetry, for all its polish and refinement, does the same.

The sun set in the sea; the same odd sun
rose from the sea,
and there was one of it and one of me.

From "Crusoe in England," *Geography III*

– W.B.

NOTES

Page

85 "Margaret and I": From a letter to Frani Blough Muser, October 22, 1933.
85 "By the time school started": From "Primer Class."
85 "Only the third": Ibid.
86 "We told each other": From "Gwendolyn."
87 "There seemed to be": From "The U.S.A. School of Writing."
87 "Miss Woodland made a model": From "The Country Mouse."
88 "We have been over to see": From a letter to Marianne Moore, May 21, 1940.
88 "The first painting": From "Gregorio Valdes."
89 "That day we bought": Ibid.
89 "Today, my dear": From a letter to Frani Blough Muser, March 11, 1941.
90 "Ancient heroes": From "Gregorio Valdes."
90 "One day she abruptly": From "Efforts of Affection."
90 "The small living room": Ibid.
91 "Well I talked to you": From a letter to Loren MacIver. July 5, 1949.
92 "There is an apple tree": From a letter to Loren MacIver, October 1950.
92 "Every night he": From "The Sea and Its Shore."
92 "Let us leave him": Ibid.
92 "One of the most effective": From "In Prison."
93 "The Biennale was": From a letter to Ilse and Kit Barker, February 5, 1954.
94 "I think Herbert Read": From a letter to Ilse and Kit Barker, February 25, 1954.
94 ". . . it has been one of my dreams": From a letter to Randall Jarrell, December 26, 1955.
95 "Another place I like": From a letter to Randall Jarrell, October 7, 1956.
95 "Uncle Neddy stands": From "Memories of Uncle Neddy."
96 "Loren [MacIver] is": From a letter to Isabella Gardner, May Day, 1957.
97 "We went to São Paulo": From a letter to Pearl Kazin, October 24, 1959.
97 "But (perhaps I've said this before)": From a letter to Robert Lowell, April 4, 1962.
98 "While we were away": From a letter to Dr. Anny Baumann, July 28, 1952.
98 "At last I am mailing you": From a letter to Dr. Anny Baumann, September 16, 1952.
99 "The cook was wonderful": From a letter to Dr. Anny Baumann, December 28, 1952.
99 "We are having": From a letter to Ilse and Kit Barker, Good Friday, 1953.
99 "The day before": From a letter to Howard Moss, September 8, 1959.
100 "Calder has left us": From a letter to Lloyd Frankenberg, March 22, 1960.
100 ". . . Carnival's one big glorious mess": From a letter to Robert Lowell, April 22, 1960.
100 "I brought back a tuba": From a letter to Dr. Anny Baumann, February 8, 1965.
101 "I did – do – like early Chirico": From a letter to U.T. and Joseph Summers, October 19, 1967.

101 "Well, off to show": From a letter to Ashley Brown, June 17, 1968.
101 "I went to the Gardner Museum": From a letter to Frani Blough Muser, January 13, 1969.
101 "You fly from Lima": From a letter to James Merrill, May 5, 1970.
102 ". . . it was a lovely": From a postcard to Robert Fizdale, January 8, 1971.
102 "Frani took me": From a letter to Loren MacIver, April 21, 1972.
102 "There is a magnificent view": From a letter to Frani Blough Muser, July 9, 1973.
102 "Yesterday I actually": From a letter to Dr. Anny Baumann, December 24, 1975.
103 "I was trying to remember": From a letter to Dorothee Bowie, January 26, 1978.
103 "I had to go to Rockland": From a letter to Dorothee Bowie, July 4, 1978.
103 "I have the most beautiful bouquet": From a letter to Dorothee Bowie, February 9, 1979.